HOLT
2
SPANISH

¡Ven conmigo!®

Student Make-Up Assignments

HOLT, RINEHART AND WINSTON

A Harcourt Classroom Education Company

Austin · New York · Orlando · Atlanta · San Francisco · Boston · Dallas · Toronto · London

Contributing Writer:

Rafael Ríos

Cover Photography Credits:
(tl), Index Stock; (c), Network Productions/Index Stock; (br), Digital Imagery® © 2003 PhotoDisc, Inc.

Photo Credits
All photos by Marty Granger/Edge Video Productions/HRW except:
106 (all), Michelle Bridwell/Frontera Fotos; 115 (bc) John Cleare/Animals Animals/Earth Scenes; (br), Billy E. Barnes; (bl), Michelle Bridwell/Frontera Fotos; 116 (tl), Myrleen Ferguson Cate/PhotoEdit; (tr, cl), Michelle Bridwell/Frontera Fotos; (cr), Billy E. Barnes; 132 (cl), ©T.L. Keith Kent/Peter Arnold, Inc.; (bl), B.L. King/H. Armstrong Roberts; (br), B.R. Reed Kaestner/Zephyr Pictures; 139 (cl) ©John Warden/Getty Images/Stone; (bl) Gerard Lacz/Animals Animals/Earth Scenes; (cr) Bob Talbot Photography; (br), T & P Leeson/Zephyr Pictures.

¡VEN CONMIGO! is a trademark licensed to Holt, Rinehart and Winston, registered in the United States of America and/or other jurisdictions.

Printed in the United States of America

ISBN 0-03-065916-7

1 2 3 4 5   066   04 03 02 01

Table of Contents

ANSWERS

To the Teacher

The blackline masters in this ancillary will help you keep track of the instructional material covered in a school year, so that you can give make-up information to students who missed class.

The first section of the book is a Diagnostic Table. In the first column of the table is a list of all the major presentations that make up the building blocks of the **Capítulo:** the functional expressions, the grammar, and the vocabulary. The activities listed in the other four columns are correlated to the **Más práctica gramatical** in the *Pupil's Edition,* the **Cuaderno de actividades,** the **Cuaderno de grámatica,** and the **Interactive CD-ROM Tutor.** This table, which gives you an overview of the presentations and opportunities for practice, can also be used as a global reference for students who need extra practice in problem areas.

The second section of the book contains the Student Make-Up Assignments Checklists. These blackline masters (one for each **paso** of the *Pupil's Edition)* can be photocopied and given to students as make-up assignments. On the left-hand side of each blackline master is a list of the presentations in each **paso.** If students missed a specific presentation (or presentations), the checklist tells them what activities they can do in the **Más práctica gramatical** in the *Pupil's Edition,* the **Cuaderno de actividades,** the **Cuaderno de grámatica,** or the **Interactive CD-ROM Tutor** to practice the material they missed when they were absent from class.

The third section of the book contains Alternative Quizzes that can be given to students who were absent from class when the regular Grammar and Vocabulary Quiz (Quiz A in the Testing Program) was given. The Alternative Quizzes could also be used in a different way: You can give both quizzes in the regular class, alternating rows, for example, so that students are not tempted to glance at their neighbor's paper.

The Alternative Quizzes were carefully built to reflect the same weight and level of difficulty as the regular quizzes, so that you can be assured that two students who take different versions of the quiz feel that they have been tested equally.

Diagnostic Information

The activities listed in this table, from the **Cuaderno de actividades, Cuaderno de gramática,** and the **Más práctica gramatical** in the *Pupil's Edition*, provide students with extra practice in problem areas.

Gramática = white background; **Vocabulario** = light gray; **Así se dice** = dark gray

CAPÍTULO 1	Más práctica gramatical	Cuaderno de gramática	Cuaderno de actividades	Interactive CD-ROM Tutor
Introducing yourself and others	Act. 1, p. 26	Acts. 1–2, p. 1	Act. 4, p. 3	Act. 1, CD 1
Describing people			Acts. 3, 6, pp. 2, 4	Act. 2, CD 1
Adjective agreement	Acts. 2–3, pp. 26–27	Acts. 3–6, pp. 2–3		Act. 3, CD 1
Vocabulario: Nationalities	Act. 3, p. 27	Acts. 7–8, p. 4	Acts. 5, 7, 18, pp. 3–4, 12	
Talking about what you and others do			Acts. 8–9, pp. 5–6	Act. 4, CD 1
Present tense of regular verbs	Act. 4, p. 27	Acts. 9–10, p. 5		Act. 5, CD 1
Saying what you like and don't like	Acts. 7–8, p. 29		Acts. 12–16, pp. 8–10	Act. 6, CD 1
CAPÍTULO 2	Más práctica gramatical	Cuaderno de gramática	Cuaderno de actividades	Interactive CD-ROM Tutor
Talking about how you're feeling		Acts. 2–3, pp. 10–11	Acts. 3–4, 6–8, pp. 14, 16	Act. 1, CD 1
Vocabulario: Emotions and moods	Act. 1, p. 54	Acts. 4–5, p. 11		
Making suggestions and responding to them	Act. 2, p. 54		Act. 5, p. 15	Act. 2, CD 1
Saying if something has already been done			Act. 9, p. 17	Act. 3, CD 1
Vocabulario: Adverbs of time		Acts. 6–7, p. 12	Act. 10, p. 17	
Preterite of regular -**ar** verbs	Act. 3, p. 55	Acts. 8–10, pp. 13–14	Act. 11, p. 18	
Asking for and offering help			Acts. 12–13, p. 19	
The stem-changing forms of **querer** and **poder**	Act. 4, p. 55	Act. 14, p. 15	Act. 14, p. 19	Act. 4, CD 1
Describing your city or town (using the verb **estar**)	Act. 5, p. 56		Acts. 15–16, pp. 20–21	Act. 6, CD 1
Vocabulario: ¿Qué tiempo hace?	Acts. 6–7, pp. 56–57	Acts. 17–18, p. 17	Acts. 17–18, p. 22	Act. 5, CD 1

CAPÍTULO 3	Más práctica gramatical	Cuaderno de gramática	Cuaderno de actividades	Interactive CD-ROM Tutor
Vocabulario: Daily routine		Acts. 1–2, p. 18	Acts. 3–6, 13, pp. 26–27, 31	
Reflexive verbs and pronouns	Act. 1, p. 86	Acts. 4–5, p. 19	Acts. 7, 11, pp. 27, 29	Act. 1, CD 1
The stem-changing forms of **vestirse**	Act. 2, p. 86	Act. 6, p. 20		Act. 2, CD 1
Talking about your daily routine			Acts. 8–9, p. 28	
Adverbs with -**mente**	Act. 3, p. 87	Act. 7, p. 20		
Vocabulario: Los quehaceres	Act. 4, p. 87	Act. 9, p. 21	Acts. 10, 13, pp. 29, 31	Act. 4, CD 1
Talking about responsibilities			Act. 12, p. 30	
Direct object pronouns: **lo, la, los, las**	Acts. 5–6, p. 88	Acts. 10–11, p. 22	Act. 14, p. 31	
Complaining		Acts. 12–13, p. 23		Act. 3, CD 1
Talking about hobbies and pastimes				Act. 5, CD 1
Vocabulario: Hobbies and pastimes	Act. 7, p. 89	Acts. 14–16, p. 24	Act. 15, p. 32	
Saying how long something has been going on	Act. 7, p. 89		Acts. 16–19, pp. 32–34	Act. 5, CD 1
Hace + amount of time + **que** + present tense	Act. 7, p. 89	Acts. 19–20, p. 26		Act. 6, CD 1

CAPÍTULO 4	Más práctica gramatical	Cuaderno de gramática	Cuaderno de actividades	Interactive CD-ROM Tutor
Asking for and giving opinions			Acts. 3–4, p. 37	Act. 1, CD 1
Giving advice			Acts. 7–8, p. 40	
The use of conditional: **deberías**		Act. 1, p. 27		
Vocabulario: En el colegio, hay que...	Act. 1, p. 116	Acts. 2–4, p. 28	Acts. 5–6, p. 39	Act. 2, CD 1
Vocabulario: More vocabulary for school	Act. 2, p. 116	Act. 5, p. 29		Act. 2, CD 1
Vocabulario: Adjetivos	Act. 3, p. 117	Act. 8, p. 30	Acts. 9–11, pp. 41–42	Act. 3, CD 1
The usage of **ser** and **estar**	Act. 4, p. 117	Acts. 9–15, pp. 30–33	Acts. 12–13, pp. 42–43	
Talking about things and people you know		Act. 16, p. 33	Act. 14, p. 43	Act. 5, CD 1
The usage of the verb **conocer**	Act. 5, p. 118	Act. 16, p. 33	Act. 14, p. 43	
Making comparisons	Act. 6, p. 118		Act. 15, p. 43	Act. 4, CD 1
Vocabulario: Hacer planes para...	Act. 7, p. 119	Act. 18, p. 34	Acts. 16–17, p. 44	Act. 6, CD1
Making plans			Act. 18, p. 45	
Direct object pronouns	Act. 8, p. 119	Acts. 19–20, pp. 34–35	Acts. 19–20, pp. 45–46	Act. 5, CD 1

Holt Spanish 2 ¡Ven conmigo!

CAPÍTULO 5	Más práctica gramatical	Cuaderno de gramática	Cuaderno de actividades	Interactive CD-ROM Tutor
Vocabulario: ¿Qué deporte te gustaría practicar?		Acts. 1–2, p. 36	Act. 3, p. 50	
Talking about staying fit and healthy				
The preterite forms of the verb **domir**	Act. 1, p. 150	Act. 3, p. 37	Act. 5, p. 51	
Vocabulario: En el gimnasio	Act. 2, p. 150	Acts. 4–5, pp. 37–38	Acts. 4, 6, pp. 50–51	Act. 1, CD 2
Preterite of -**er** and -**ir** verbs	Act. 3, p. 151	Acts. 6–7, p. 38	Act. 7, p. 52	Act. 2, CD 2
Telling someone what to do and not to do			Act. 9, p. 53	Act. 4, CD 2
Vocabulario: Well-being		Acts. 10–11, p. 40	Acts. 8, 10, pp. 53–54	
Informal commands	Act. 4, p. 151	Act. 12, p. 41	Act. 12, p. 55	Act. 3, CD 2
Jugar and **practicar** in negative commands	Act. 5, p. 152			
Irregular informal commands	Act. 4, p. 151	Acts. 13–14, p. 42	Act. 11, p. 54	Act. 3, CD 2
Giving explanations			Act. 13, p. 56	Act. 5, CD 2
The preterite forms of **poder**	Act. 6, p. 152	Act. 15, p. 43	Act. 14, p. 57	
Vocabulario: Parts of the body and some useful verbs		Acts. 16–17, p. 43	Acts. 15–17, pp. 57–58	Act. 6 CD 2
Vocabulario: More verbs		Act. 18, p. 44		
The usage of reflexive verbs	Act. 7, p. 153	Act. 19, p. 44		

CAPÍTULO 6	Más práctica gramatical	Cuaderno de gramática	Cuaderno de actividades	Interactive CD-ROM Tutor
Vocabulario: The city	Act. 1, p. 178	Acts. 1–2, p. 45	Act. 2, p. 62	Act. 1, CD 2
Asking for and giving information			Acts. 3–4, pp. 62–63	
The present tense forms of **saber**	Act. 2, p. 178	Acts. 3–5, p. 46	Act. 5, p. 63	Act. 2, CD 2
Saber vs. **conocer**	Acts. 3–4, p. 179	Acts. 6–7, p. 47	Acts. 6–7, p. 64	Act. 2, CD 2
Vocabulario: Useful words for sight seeing			Acts. 8–9, p. 65	
Relating a series of events	Act. 5, p. 180	Acts. 10, 12–13, pp. 49–50	Acts. 10–12, pp. 66–67	Act. 3, CD 2
Vocabulario: Useful words for travelers	Act. 6, p. 180	Acts. 8–9, p. 48		
Ordering at a restaurant			Act. 13, p. 68	Act. 5, CD 2
Vocabulario: En el restaurante		Act. 14, p. 51		Act. 6, CD 2
Preterite forms of **pedir** and **servir**	Act. 7, p. 181	Act. 15, p. 51	Act. 14, p. 69	Act. 4, CD 2
The verb **traer**	Acts. 7–8, p. 181	Acts. 16–18, 21, pp. 52–53	Acts. 15–16, pp. 69–70	

CAPÍTULO 7	Más práctica gramatical	Cuaderno de gramática	Cuaderno de actividades	Interactive CD-ROM Tutor
Talking about what you used to do			Act. 3, p. 74	
The imperfect tense	Act. 1, p. 212	Acts. 1–5, pp. 54–55	Acts. 4–5, p. 74	Act. 2, CD 2
The verbs **ir** and **ver**	Act. 2, p. 212	Act. 6, p. 56		Act. 2, CD 2
Vocabulario: Useful verbs in the park	Act. 3, p. 213	Act. 7, p. 56		Act. 1, CD 2
Saying what you used to like and dislike			Acts. 6–7, pp. 75–76	
Changes to conjunctions	Act. 4, pp. 213–214	Acts. 8–9, p. 57		
Describing what people and things were like			Act. 9, p. 78	
Vocabulario: Adjectives		Acts. 12–13, p. 59	Act. 8, p. 77	Act. 4, CD 2
The imperfect of the verb **ser**	Act. 5, p. 214	Acts. 10–11, 19, pp. 58, 61	Act. 10, p. 78	
Vocabulario: More words to talk about the city		Acts. 14–15, p. 60	Act. 11, p. 79	Act. 5, CD 2
The imperfect form of **hay**	Act. 6, p. 214	Acts. 17–18, p. 61	Act. 12, p. 79	Act. 3, CD 2
Vocabulario: More vocabulary		Act. 16, p. 60	Act. 16, p. 81	
Using comparisons to describe people			Acts. 13, 15, pp. 80–81	
Comparisons of equality	Acts. 7–8, p. 215	Acts. 20–23, pp. 62–63	Acts. 14, 17, pp. 80, 82	Act. 6, CD 2

CAPÍTULO 8	Más práctica gramatical	Cuaderno de gramática	Cuaderno de actividades	Interactive CD-ROM Tutor
Describing a past event			Act. 3, p. 86	Act. 1, CD 2
The usage of **-isimo/a**	Act. 1, p. 240	Acts. 1–2, p. 64	Acts. 4, 6, pp. 86, 88	
Vocabulario: En el zoológico		Acts. 3–4, p. 65	Act. 5, p. 87	Act. 2, CD 2
Superlatives	Act. 2, p. 240	Acts. 5–7, pp. 65–66	Act. 7, p. 88	Act. 3, CD 2
Vocabulario: Hacer un mandado	Act. 3, p. 241	Acts. 8–9, p. 67		Act. 5, CD 2
Saying why you couldn't do something			Acts. 8–10, pp. 89–91	
The usage of prepositions after some verbs	Act. 4, p. 241	Acts. 10–11, p. 68		
Mientras and the imperfect form of the verb	Act. 5, p. 242	Acts. 12–13, p. 69	Act. 11, p. 91	Act. 4, CD 2
Reporting what someone said			Acts. 12, 15, p. 92	
Vocabulario: En el festival		Acts. 14–15, p. 70	Act. 13, p. 92	
Decir in the preterite	Acts. 6–7, pp. 242-243	Acts. 16–17, p. 71	Acts. 14, 16, pp. 93–94	Act. 6, CD 2

CAPÍTULO 9	Más práctica gramatical	Cuaderno de gramática	Cuaderno de actividades	Interactive CD-ROM Tutor
Asking for and giving directions				Act. 2, CD 3
Vocabulario: Useful verbs to give directions	Act. 1, p. 274	Acts. 1–2, p. 72	Acts. 3–6, pp. 98–100	Act. 1, CD 3
Formal commands (singular and plural)	Acts. 2–3, p. 275	Acts. 3–7, pp. 73–75	Act. 7, p. 100	Act. 3, CD 3
Vocabulario: En la tienda de ropa		Acts. 8–10, pp. 76	Act. 8, p. 101	Act. 4, CD 3
Asking for help in a store			Act. 9, p. 101	Act. 6, CD 3
Talking about how clothes look and fit	Act. 4, p. 276		Acts. 10, 12, 19, pp. 102, 103, 108	Act. 5, CD 3
Bargaining in a market			Acts. 13–14, 16, pp. 104–106	Act. 6, CD 3
Vocabulario: More vocabulary for the store	Act. 6, p. 277	Acts. 12–13, pp. 78–79	Act. 15, p. 105	
Se te ha olvidado? Direct objects	Act. 7, p. 277			

CAPÍTULO 10	Más práctica gramatical	Cuaderno de gramática	Cuaderno de actividades	Interactive CD-ROM Tutor
Setting the scene for a story			Acts. 3–4, pp. 110–111	
Vocabulario: The weather	Act. 1, p. 304	Acts. 1–2, p. 80		
Preterite and imperfect contrasted	Acts. 2–3, p. 305	Acts. 4–7, pp. 81–82	Acts. 5–6, p. 112	Act. 2, CD 3
Vocabulario: More reflexive verbs		Act. 8, p. 83		Act. 1, CD 3
The preterite form of oír, **creer, leer,** and **caerse**	Act. 3, p. 305	Act. 9, p. 83		Act. 2, CD 3
Continuing and ending a story		Acts. 7–8, p. 82	Acts. 7–8, p. 113	Act. 4, CD 3
Vocabulario: Ciencia ficción y cuentos de hadas	Act. 4, p. 306	Acts. 10–11, p. 84	Act. 10, p. 114	Act. 5, CD 3
Preterite and imperfect to tell a story	Act. 5, p. 306	Acts. 12–15, pp. 85–86	Acts. 9, 11–12, pp. 114–115	Act. 3, CD 3
Vocabulario: Las noticias	Act. 6, p. 307	Acts. 16–17, p. 87	Acts. 13–14, pp. 116–117	
Talking about the latest news		Act. 19, p. 88	Acts. 15–16, pp. 117–118	Act. 6, CD 3
Reacting to news			Act. 17, p. 118	Act. 6, CD 3
The preterite forms of the verb **tener**	Act. 7, p. 307	Act. 18, p. 88		

CAPÍTULO 11	Más práctica gramatical	Cuaderno de gramática	Cuaderno de actividades	Interactive CD-ROM Tutor
Vocabulario: El medio ambiente		Acts. 1–2, p. 89	Acts. 3–4, pp. 122–123	Act. 1, CD 3
Describing a problem	Act. 1, p. 338		Act. 5, p. 123	Act. 4, CD 3
The usage of the negative	Act. 2, p. 338	Acts. 3–5, pp. 90–91	Act. 6, p. 124	Act. 2, CD 3
Vocabulario: La naturaleza	Act. 3, p. 339	Acts. 6–7, p. 91	Acts. 7–8, pp. 124–125	Act. 1, CD 3
Talking about consequences	Act. 3, p. 339	Act. 8, p. 92	Acts. 9–10, pp. 125–126	Act. 4, CD 3
Expressing agreement and disagreement	Act. 5, p. 340	Acts. 9–11, pp. 92–93	Acts. 11–12, pp. 126–127	Act. 3, CD 3
Talking about obligations and solutions			Acts. 13–14, p. 128	
Vocabulario: Tú puedes...		Acts. 14–15, p. 95	Acts. 15–16, p. 129	Act. 6, CD 3
The usage of the word **si**	Act. 6, p. 340	Acts. 16–17, pp. 95–96	Act. 17, p. 130	
Nosotros commands	Act. 7, p. 341	Acts. 18–20, pp. 96–97	Act. 18, p. 130	Act. 5, CD 3

CAPÍTULO 12	Más práctica gramatical	Cuaderno de gramática	Cuaderno de actividades	Interactive CD-ROM Tutor
Vocabulario: Writing letters		Acts. 1–3, pp. 98–99	Act. 2, p. 134	
Exchanging the latest news			Acts. 4–5, p. 135	Act. 1, CD 3
Talking about where you went and what you did	Acts. 1–3, pp. 364–365			Act. 3, CD 3
Vocabulario: Actividades		Acts. 4–5, p. 99	Act. 3, p. 134	Act. 2, CD 3
Telling when something happened			Act. 6, p. 136	
Saying how you feel about people	Act. 4, p. 365		Acts. 7–10, pp. 137–139	Act. 4, CD 3
Se te ha olvidado? The imperfect	Act. 5, p. 366			
Describing places	Act. 6, p. 366		Act. 11, p. 139	Act. 4, CD 3
Saying when you're going to do something		Acts. 15–16, p. 104	Acts. 12, 16, pp. 140, 142	Act. 6, CD 3
Vocabulario: Cuando...			Acts. 13–15, pp. 140–141	
The subjunctive	Act. 7, p. 367	Acts. 20–21, p. 106		

Holt Spanish 2 ¡Ven conmigo!

STUDENT MAKE-UP ASSIGNMENTS CHECKLIST

CAPÍTULO 1

Mis amigos y yo

■ PRIMER PASO Student Make-Up Assignments Checklist

Pupil's Edition, pp. 9–12

Study the expressions in the **Así se dice** box on page 9: introducing yourself and others. You should know how to introduce yourself and others.	☐ Do Activity 6, p. 9. ☐ Do Activity 7, p. 9 as a writing activity. Write a paragraph introducing yourself to a new classmate. ☐ For additional practice, do Activity 4, p. 3 in the **Cuaderno de actividades.** ☐ For additional practice, do Activities 1–2, p. 1 in the **Cuaderno de gramática.** ☐ For additional practice, do Activity 1, CD 1 in the **Interactive CD-ROM Tutor.**
Study the expressions in the **Así se dice** box on page 10: describing people. You should know how to describe people.	☐ Do Activity 14, p. 24 as a writing activity. ☐ For additional practice, do Activities 3, 6, pp. 2, 4 in the **Cuaderno de actividades.** ☐ For additional practice, do Activity 2, CD 1 in the **Interactive CD-ROM Tutor.**
Study the grammar presentation in the **Gramática** box on page 11: adjective agreement.	☐ Do Activity 9, p. 11. ☐ Do Activity 10, p. 11. ☐ Do Activity 11, p. 11 as a writing activity. ☐ For additional practice, do Activities 2-3, pp. 26-27 in **Más práctica gramatical.** ☐ For additional practice, do Activities 3–6, pp. 2–3 in the **Cuaderno de gramática.** ☐ For additional practice, do Activity 3, CD 1 in the **Interactive CD-ROM Tutor.**
Study the expressions in the **Vocabulario** box on page 12.	☐ Do Activity 12, p. 12 as a writing activity. ☐ Do Activity 13, p. 12 as a writing activity. Write the description of six famous people. ☐ Do Activity 14, p. 12. ☐ For additional practice, do Activity 3, p. 27 in **Más práctica gramatical.**

CAPÍTULO 1

☐ For additional practice, do Activities 5, 7, 18, pp. 3–4, 12 in the **Cuaderno de actividades.**

☐ For additional practice, do Activities 7–8, p. 4 in the **Cuaderno de gramática.**

PRIMER PASO Self-Test

Can you introduce yourself and others?	How would you introduce the following people to a friend?
	1. your teacher
	2. your best friend
	3. your father or guardian
	4. Maribel
	5. Pablo
	6. yourself
Can you describe people?	Maribel is describing herself, her friends, and her parents. How would she say that...?
	1. she is Spanish
	2. Pablo and Enrique are 16 years old
	3. her father has white hair and wears glasses
	4. her mother is of medium height
	5. Verónica and Pilar are very friendly

For an **online self-test,** go to **go.hrw.com.**

WV3 ANDALUCIA-1

CAPÍTULO

1 Mis amigos y yo

■ SEGUNDO PASO Student Make-Up Assignments Checklist

Pupil's Edition, pp. 14–18

Study the expressions in the **Así se dice** box on page 15: talking about what you and others do. You should know how to talk about what you and others do.	☐ For additional practice, do Activities 5–6, pp. 8–9 in the **Cuaderno de actividades.** ☐ For additional practice, do Activity 4, CD 1 in the **Interactive CD-ROM Tutor.**
Study the grammar presentation in the **Gramática** box on page 16: present tense of regular verbs.	☐ Do Activity 17, p. 16, as a writing activity. Write six questions as directed, then answer them. ☐ Do Activity 18, p. 16, as a writing activity. ☐ Do Activity 19, p. 17, as a writing activity. ☐ Do Activity 20, p. 17, as a writing activity. ☐ Do Activity 21, p. 17, as a writing activity. ☐ Do Activity 22, p. 18, as a writing activity. ☐ Do Activity 23, p. 18, as a writing activity. ☐ Do Activity 24, p. 18. ☐ For additional practice, do Activity 4, p. 27 in **Más práctica gramatical.** ☐ For additional practice, do Activities 9–10, p. 5 in the **Cuaderno de gramática.** ☐ For additional practice, do Activity 5, CD 1 in the **Interactive CD-ROM Tutor.**

CAPÍTULO 1

SEGUNDO PASO Self-Test

Can you talk about what you and others do?	Maribel and her friends like to do a lot of different things on the weekend. How would you say that . . . ?

1. Maribel runs in the park

2. Pablo plays soccer

3. Verónica plays tennis

4. Pilar and Enrique study in the library

5. Robertín eats pizza

6. Maribel and Robertín swim in the pool

7. Pilar plays video games

8. Mr. Rojas works

José Luis and his friends are planning an exciting weekend. What are they going to do in the following places?

1. María Inés/la biblioteca

2. Juan y Alejandro/el restaurante

3. Paco y yo/la librería

4. Laura/el parque

5. yo/la playa

6. tú/la casa

 For an **online self-test**, go to **go.hrw.com**.

WV3 ANDALUCIA-1

Holt Spanish 2 ¡Ven conmigo!, Chapter 1

CAPÍTULO

1

Mis amigos y yo

■ **TERCER PASO** Student Make-Up Assignments Checklist

Pupil's Edition, pp. 32–35

Study the expressions in the **Así se dice** box on page 32: talking about likes and dislikes. You should know how to ask what a friend likes and understand the answer.	☐ Do Activity 29, p. 32.
	☐ Do Activity 28, p. 22, as a writing activity.
	☐ Do Activity 29, p. 22, as a writing activity.
	☐ Do Activity 30, p. 22, as a writing activity. Write about what you like and don't like and why.
	☐ Do Activity 31, p. 23, as a writing activity. Write about which person would be a better pen pal for you and why.
	☐ Do Activity 32, p. 23.
	☐ For additional practice, do Activity 8–9, p. 39 in **Más práctica gramatical.**
	☐ For additional practice, do Activity 7, pp. 16–17 in the **Cuaderno de gramática.**
	☐ For additional practice, do Activity 6, CD 1 in the **Interactive CD-ROM Tutor.**
Study the grammar presentation in the **Gramática** box on page 33: nouns and definite articles.	☐ Do Activity 30, p. 33.
	☐ For additional practice, do Activity 8, pp. 18–20 in the **Cuaderno de gramática.**
	☐ For additional practice, do Activity 9, p. 39 in **Más práctica gramatical.**

◼ TERCER PASO Self-Test

Can you say what you like and don't like?	Use **gustar, fascinar, encantar,** or **chocar** to tell how you feel about the following things. Then tell how a friend or relative feels about each thing.

Use **gustar, fascinar, encantar,** or **chocar** to tell how you feel about the following things. Then tell how a friend or relative feels about each thing.

1. jugar al fútbol
2. la comida mexicana
3. los videojuegos
4. visitar museos
5. las películas de terror
6. estudiar los sábados
7. salir con amigos
8. la playa
9. leer novelas
10. las ciencias

For an **online self-test**, go to **go.hrw.com**.

WV3 ANDALUCIA-1

Holt Spanish 2 ¡Ven conmigo!, Chapter 1

CAPÍTULO 2 — Un viaje al extranjero

■ PRIMER PASO Student Make-Up Assignments Checklist

Pupil's Edition, pp. 39–41

Study the expressions in the **Así se dice** box on page 40: talking about how you're feeling. You should know how to talk about how you're feeling.	☐ Do Activity 7, p.40, as a writing activity. ☐ For additional practice, do Activities 3–4, 6–8, pp. 14–16 in the **Cuaderno de actividades.** ☐ For additional practice, do Activities 2–3, pp. 10–11 in the **Cuaderno de gramática.** ☐ For additional practice, do Activity 1, CD 1 in the **Interactive CD-ROM Tutor.**
Study the expressions in the **Vocabulario** box on page 40.	☐ Do Activity 8, p. 40. ☐ For additional practice, do Activities 4–5, p. 11 in the **Cuaderno de gramática.**
Study the expressions in the **Así se dice** box on page 41: making suggestions and responding to them. You should know how to make suggestions and respond to them.	☐ Do Activity 10, p. 41, as a writing activity. ☐ Do Activity 11, p. 41. ☐ For additional practice, do Activity 5, p. 15 in the **Cuaderno de actividades.** ☐ For additional practice, do Activity 2, CD 1 in the **Interactive CD-ROM Tutor.**

CAPÍTULO 2

■ PRIMER PASO Self-Test

Can you talk about how you're feeling?	Look at the pictures in **A ver si puedo...** on page 60. How would these people describe how they're feeling?
	1. Maribel
	2. Manuel
	3. Félix and Gustavo
	4. Norma

 For an **online self-test**, go to **go.hrw.com**.

WV3 ANDALUCIA-2

CAPÍTULO 2

Holt Spanish 2 ¡Ven conmigo!, Chapter 2

2 Un viaje al extranjero

■ SEGUNDO PASO Student Make-Up Assignments Checklist

Pupil's Edition, pp. 42–46

Study the expressions in the **Así se dice** box on page 42: saying if something has already been done. You should know how to say if something has already been done.	☐ For additional practice, do Activity 9, p. 17 in the **Cuaderno de actividades**. ☐ For additional practice, do Activity 3, CD 1 in the **Interactive CD-ROM Tutor**.
Study the expressions in the **Vocabulario** box on page 42: **Hoy es domingo. ¿Cuándo lo hiciste?**	☐ Do Activity 14, p. 43, as a writing activity. Rewrite the sentences. ☐ For additional practice, do Activity 10, p. 7 in the **Cuaderno de actividades**. ☐ For additional practice, do Activities 6–7, p. 12 in the **Cuaderno de ejercicios**.
Study the grammar presentation in the **Gramática** box on page 43: preterite of regular -**ar** verbs.	☐ Do Activity 15, p. 44. ☐ Do Activity 16, p. 44, as a writing activity. ☐ Do Activity 17, p. 45. ☐ Do Activity 18, p. 45. ☐ Do Activity 19, p. 45. ☐ Do Activity 20, p. 45. ☐ For additional practice, do Activity 3, p. 55 in **Más práctica gramatical**. ☐ For additional practice, do Activity 11, p. 11 in the **Cuaderno de actividades**. ☐ For additional practice, do Activities 8–10, pp. 13–14 in the **Cuaderno de gramática**.
Study the expressions in the **Así se dice** box on page 46: asking for and offering help. You should know how to ask for and offer help.	☐ For additional practice, do Activities 12–13, p. 19 in the **Cuaderno de actividades**.
Study the grammar presentation in the **Nota gramatical** box on page 46: **e → ie; o → ue.**	☐ Do Activity 22, p. 46, as a writing activity. ☐ Do Activity 23, p. 46. ☐ For additional practice, do Activity 4, p. 55 in **Más práctica gramatical**.

CAPÍTULO 2

☐ For additional practice, do Activity 14, p. 19 in the **Cuaderno de actividades.**

☐ For additional practice, do Activity 14, p. 15 in the **Cuaderno de gramática.**

☐ For additional practice, do Activity 4, CD 1 in the **Interactive CD-ROM Tutor.**

■ SEGUNDO PASO Self-Test

CAPÍTULO 2

Can you make suggestions and respond to them?	Maribel is nervous because she's going to study abroad. Make the following suggestions to help her relax. Then say how she might respond, using the cues in parentheses.
	1. ir al cine (no, ocupada)
	2. salir con amigos (no, cansada)
	3. leer una novela (sí, buena idea)
	4. escuchar música clásica (sí, buena idea)
	5. hacer la maleta (no, nerviosa)
	6. escribir una carta a la nueva familia (sí, buena idea)
Can you say if something has already been done?	How would you ask someone if each thing on the list below has already been done?
	✓ lavar ropa ✓ comprar el billete de avión limpiar el cuarto hacer la maleta ✓ ir al banco How would that person answer?
Can you ask for and offer help?	How would you ask for or offer help in the following situations?
	1. Your friend has lost his or her passport.
	2. You're running late but you still have to pack.
	3. Your aunt has just asked you to help her.
	4. You see an elderly lady carrying a heavy suitcase.
	5. You need help with your homework.

 For an **online self-test**, go to **go.hrw.com.**

WV3 ANDALUCIA-2

CAPÍTULO

2

Un viaje al extranjero

■ TERCER PASO Student Make-Up Assignments Checklist

Pupil's Edition, pp. 49–51

Study the expressions in the **Así se dice** box on page 49: describing your city or town. You should know how to describe your city or town.	☐ Do Activity 26, p. 45, as a writing activity. ☐ Do Activity 27, p. 46, as a writing activity. ☐ For additional practice, do Activity 5, p. 56 in **Más práctica gramatical.** ☐ For additional practice, do Activities 15–16, pp. 20–21 in the **Cuaderno de actividades.** ☐ For additional practice, do Activity 6, CD 1 in the **Interactive CD-ROM Tutor.**
Study the grammar expressions in the **Vocabulario** box on page 46: **¿Qué tiempo hace?**	☐ Do Activity 28, p. 50, as a writing activity. ☐ Do Activity 29, p. 50. ☐ Do Activity 30, p. 51, as a writing activity. ☐ Do Activity 31, p. 51, as a writing activity. ☐ Do Activity 32, p. 51. ☐ For additional practice, do Activities 17–18, p. 22 in the **Cuaderno de actividades.** ☐ For additional practice, do Activities 17–18, p. 17 in the **Cuaderno de gramática.** ☐ For additional practice, do Activity 5, CD 1 in the **Interactive CD-ROM Tutor.**

CAPÍTULO 2

◼ TERCER PASO Self-Test

Can you describe your city or town?	Describe the following places:
	1. Sevilla, España
	2. tu ciudad en el verano
	3. tu ciudad en el invierno
	4. la ciudad ideal

 For an **online self-test**, go to **go.hrw.com**.

WV3 ANDALUCIA-2

CAPÍTULO 2

CAPÍTULO 3

3 La vida cotidiana

■ PRIMER PASO Student Make-Up Assignments Checklist

Pupil's Edition, pp. 71–74.

Study the expressions in the **Vocabulario** box on page 71.	☐ Do Activity 6, p. 71, as a writing activity. ☐ For additional practice, do Activities 3–6, 13, pp. 26–27, 31 in the **Cuaderno de actividades**. ☐ For additional practice, do Activities 1–2, p. 18 in the **Cuaderno de gramática**.
Study the grammar presentation in the **Gramática** box on page 72: reflexive verbs and pronouns.	☐ Do Activity 8, p. 65. ☐ For additional practice, do Activity 1, p. 86 in **Más práctica gramatical**. ☐ For additional practice, do Activities 7, 11, pp. 27, 29 in the **Cuaderno de actividades**. ☐ For additional practice, do Activities 4–5, p. 19 in the **Cuaderno de gramática**. ☐ For additional practice, do Activity 1, CD 1 in the **Interactive CD-ROM Tutor**.
Study the grammar presentation in the **Nota gramatical** box on page 73: **e ➔ i**.	☐ For additional practice, do Activity 2, p. 86 in **Más práctica gramatical**. ☐ For additional practice, do Activity 6, p. 20 in the **Cuaderno de gramática**. ☐ For additional practice, do Activity 2, CD 1 in the **Interactive CD-ROM Tutor**.
Study the expressions in the **Así se dice** box on page 73: talking about your daily routine. You should know how to talk about your daily routine.	☐ Do Activity 9, p. 73 as a writing activity. ☐ For additional practice, do Activities 8–9, p. 28 in the **Cuaderno de actividades**.
Study the grammar presentation in the **Nota gramatical** box on page 74: adverbs.	☐ Do Activity 10, p. 74, as a writing activity. ☐ Do Activity 11, p. 74, as a writing activity. ☐ Do Activity 12, p. 74. ☐ Do Activity 13, p. 74. ☐ For additional practice, do Activity 3, p. 87 in **Más práctica gramatical**. ☐ For additional practice, do Activity 7, p. 20 in the **Cuaderno de gramática**.

CAPÍTULO 3

PRIMER PASO Self-Test

Can you talk about your daily routine?	Look at the drawings in Activity 1 on the **A ver si puedo...** page in your textbook (p. 92), and describe what these people are doing.

1. Esteban

2. Alfonso

3. Susana

4. Deion

Use -**mente** adverbs to describe how the people in the drawings in Activity 1, p. 92, do each activity.

 For an **online self-test**, go to **go.hrw.com**.

WV3 Mexico–3

Holt Spanish 2 ¡Ven conmigo!, Chapter 3

CAPÍTULO 3

CAPÍTULO

3 La vida cotidiana

■ SEGUNDO PASO Student Make-Up Assignments Checklist

Pupil's Edition, pp. 76–79

Study the expressions in the **Vocabulario** box on page 76: **Los quehaceres.**	☐ Do Activity 14, p. 76. ☐ For additional practice, do Activities 10, 13, pp. 29, 31 in the **Cuaderno de actividades.** ☐ For additional practice, do Activity 9, p. 21 in the **Cuaderno de gramática.** ☐ For additional practice, do Activity 4, CD 1 in the **Interactive CD-ROM Tutor.**
Study the expressions in the **Así se dice** box on page 77: talking about responsibilities. You should know how to talk about responsibilities.	☐ Do Activity 16, p. 77, as a writing activity. ☐ Do Activity 17, p. 77, as a writing activity. ☐ For additional practice, do Activity 12, p. 30 in the **Cuaderno de actividades.**
Study the grammar presentation in the **Gramática** box on page 77: object pronouns **lo, la, los, las.**	☐ Do Activity 18, p. 77, as a writing activity. ☐ For additional practice, do Activities 5–6, p. 88 in **Más práctica gramatical.** ☐ For additional practice, do Activity 14, p. 31 in the **Cuaderno de actividades.** ☐ For additional practice, do Activities 10–11, p. 22 in the **Cuaderno de gramática.**
Study the expressions in the **Así se dice** box on page 78: complaining. You should know how to complain.	☐ Do Activity 20, p. 78. ☐ Do Activity 21, p. 79 as a writing activity. ☐ Do Activity 22, p. 79 as a writing activity. ☐ Do Activity 23, p. 79. ☐ For additional practice, do Activities 12–13, p. 23 in the **Cuaderno de gramática.** ☐ For additional practice, do Activity 3, CD 1 in the **Interactive CD-ROM Tutor.**

CAPÍTULO 3

■ SEGUNDO PASO Self-Test

Can you talk about responsibilities?	Using an appropriate verb and the cues in parentheses, explain whose responsibility it is to do the household chores.
	1. las camas (tú)
	2. la mesa (yo)
	3. la sala (Ana María)
	4. el gato (Lupita)
	5. las plantas (tú)
	6. el cuarto de baño (Andrés)
Can you complain?	Imagine somebody tells you to do the following things. How would you complain?
	1. Tienes que ordenar tu cuarto.
	2. ¿Qué tal si riegas el jardín esta tarde?
	3. Necesitas barrer el piso.
	4. ¿Me puedes ayudar a sacudir el polvo?
	5. ¿Cuándo vas a tender tu cama?
	6. Te toca a tí tender las camas.

 For an **online self-test**, go to **go.hrw.com**.

WV3 Mexico–3

C A P Í T U L O   3

CAPÍTULO

3 La vida cotidiana

■ TERCER PASO Student Make-Up Assignments Checklist

Pupil's Edition, pp. 80–83

Study the expressions in the **Así se dice** box on page 81: talking about hobbies and pastimes. You should know how to talk about hobbies and pastimes.	☐ For additional practice, do Activity 5, CD 1 in the **Interactive CD-ROM Tutor.**
Study the expressions in the **Vocabulario** box on page 81.	☐ Do Activity 26, p. 82, as a writing activity. ☐ Do Activity 27, p. 82, as a writing activity. Write complete sentences telling what your favorite pastimes are. ☐ For additional practice, do Activities 7–8, p. 89 in **Más práctica gramatical.** ☐ For additional practice, do Activity 15, p. 32 in the **Cuaderno de actividades.** ☐ For additional practice, do Activities 14–16, p. 24 in the **Cuaderno de gramática.**
Study the expressions in the **Así se dice** box on page 82: saying how long something has been going on. You should know how to say how long something has been going on.	☐ Do Activity 28, p. 82, as a writing activity. ☐ For additional practice, do Activities 16–19, pp. 32–34 in the **Cuaderno de actividades.** ☐ For additional practice, do Activity 5, CD 1 in the **Interactive CD-ROM Tutor.**
Study the grammar presentation in the **Nota gramatical** box on page 82: **Hace** + amount of time + **que** + present tense.	☐ Do Activity 29, p. 83, as a writing activity. ☐ Do Activity 30, p. 83, as a writing activity. ☐ Do Activity 31, p. 83. ☐ For additional practice, do Activity 7, p. 89 in **Más práctica gramatical.** ☐ For additional practice, do Activities 19–20, p. 26 in the **Cuaderno de gramática.** ☐ For additional practice, do Activity 6, CD 1 in the **Interactive CD-ROM Tutor.**

CAPÍTULO 3

◼ TERCER PASO Self-Test

Can you talk about hobbies and pastimes?	Look at the pictures in Activity 5 in **A ver si puedo...** on page 92 in your textbook and say if you like or dislike the pastimes suggested by the pictures.
Can you say how long something has been going on?	How would you ask how long the following people have been doing the following activities? How would they answer? 1. Lupita/tocar el piano/mucho tiempo 2. Andrés/trabajar en mecánica/dos semanas 3. Mónica/despertarse a las seis/tres meses 4. Carlos y Sergio/hacer monopatín/cuatro años

 For an **online self-test**, go to **go.hrw.com**.

WV3 Mexico–3

CAPÍTULO

4 ¿Qué haces esta tarde?

■ PRIMER PASO Student Make-Up Assignments Checklist

Pupil's Edition, pp. 99–103

Study the expressions in the **Así se dice** box on page 100: asking for and giving opinions. You should know how to ask for and give opinions.	☐ Do Activity 8, p. 100, as a writing activity. ☐ Do Activity 9, p. 101, as a writing activity. ☐ Do Activity 10, p. 101, as a writing activity. ☐ For additional practice, do Activities 3–4, p. 37 in the **Cuaderno de actividades**. ☐ For additional practice, do Activity 1, CD 1 in the **Interactive CD-ROM Tutor**.
Study the grammar presentation in the **Nota gramatical** box on page 101.	☐ For additional practice, do Activity 17, p. 27 in the **Cuaderno de gramática**.
Study the expressions in the **Así se dice** box on page 101: giving advice. You should know how to give advice.	☐ For additional practice, do Activities 7–8, p. 40 in the **Cuaderno de actividades**.
Study the expressions in the **Vocabulario** box on page 101: **En el colegio hay que...**	☐ Do Activity 12, p. 102, as a writing activity. ☐ For additional practice, do Activity 1, p. 116 in **Más práctica gramatical.** ☐ For additional practice, do Activities 5–6, p. 39 in the **Cuaderno de actividades.** ☐ For additional practice, do Activities 2–4, p. 28 in the **Cuaderno de gramática.**
Study the expressions in the **Vocabulario** box on page 103.	☐ Do Activity 13, p. 103 ☐ Do Activity 14, p. 103, as a writing activity. ☐ Do Activity 15, p. 103, as a writing activity. Write a conversation. ☐ Do Activity 16, p. 103. ☐ For additional practice, do Activity 5, p. 29 in the **Cuaderno de gramática.** ☐ For additional practice, do Activity 2, CD 1 in the **Interactive CD-ROM Tutor.**

CAPÍTULO 4

■ PRIMER PASO Self-Test

Can you ask for and give opinions?	How would you ask for someone's opinion about the following people? How would you give yours?
	1. Rosie Perez
	2. Andy García
	3. tu mejor amigo o amiga
	4. el profesor o la profesora de álgebra
	5. el presidente de los Estados Unidos
Can you give advice?	Your younger friend is going to start high school next year. Make five recommendations about what your friend should do if she or he wants to succeed in high school.

 For an **online self-test**, go to **go.hrw.com**.

WV3 Mexico–4

Holt Spanish 2 ¡Ven conmigo!, Chapter 4

CAPÍTULO 4

¡Adelante con los estudios!

■ SEGUNDO PASO Student Make-Up Assignments Checklist

Pupil's Edition, pp. 104–108

Study the expressions in the **Vocabulario** box on page 105.	☐ Do Activity 19, p. 105, as a writing activity. Write a short description for each person.
	☐ For additional practice, do Activities 9–11, pp. 41–42 in the **Cuaderno de actividades**.
	☐ For additional practice, do Activity 8, p. 30 in the **Cuaderno de gramática**.
	☐ For additional practice, do Activity 3, CD 1 in the **Interactive CD-ROM Tutor**.
Study the grammar presentation in the **Nota gramatical** box on page 105: **ser** and **estar**.	☐ Do Activity 20, p. 105, as a writing activity.
	☐ For additional practice, do Activity 4, p. 117 in **Más práctica gramatical**.
	☐ For additional practice, do Activities 12–13, pp. 42–43 in the **Cuaderno de actividades**.
	☐ For additional practice, do Activities 9–15, pp. 30–33 in the **Cuaderno de gramática**.
Study the expressions in the **Así se dice** box on page 106: talking about things and people you know. You should know how to talk about things and people you know.	☐ For additional practice, do Activity 16, p. 33 in the **Cuaderno de gramática**.
	☐ For additional practice, do Activities 14, p. 43 in the **Cuaderno de actividades**.
	☐ For additional practice, do Activity 5, CD 1 in the **Interactive CD-ROM Tutor**.
Study the grammar presentation in the **Nota gramatical** box on page 106: **conocer**.	☐ Do Activity 21, p. 106, as a writing activity. Write out sentences using the clues in the exercise.
	☐ For additional practice, do Activity 5, p. 118 in **Más práctica gramatical**.
	☐ For additional practice, do Activity 14, p. 43 in the **Cuaderno de actividades**.
	☐ For additional practice, do Activity 16, p. 33 in the **Cuaderno de gramática**.

CAPÍTULO 4

Study the expressions in the **Así se dice** box on page 107: making comparisons. You should know how to make comparisons.

☐ Do Activity 24, p. 107, as a writing activity.

☐ Do Activity 25, p. 108.

☐ Do Activity 26, p. 108, as a writing activity.

☐ Do Activity 27, p. 108.

☐ For additional practice, do Activity 6, p. 118 in **Más práctica gramatical.**

☐ For additional practice, do Activity 15, p. 43 in the **Cuaderno de actividades.**

☐ For additional practice, do Activity 4, CD 1 in the **Interactive CD-ROM Tutor.**

■ SEGUNDO PASO Self-Test

Can you talk about things and people you know?

How would you ask someone if he or she knows the following people? How would you identify them? Use the drawings in Activity 3 in **A ver si puedo...** on page 122 in your textbook to describe them and tell where they are.

1. Yukari
2. Elena
3. Rafael
4. Javier
5. Roberto
6. Benjamín

Can you make comparisons?

Using the drawings in Activity 3 on the **A ver si puedo...** on page 122 in your textbook, compare the following people.

1. Roberto y Elena
2. Rafael y Juanito
3. Yukari y Benjamín
4. el abuelo Miguel y Javier

For an **online self-test**, go to go.hrw.com.

WV3 Mexico–4

CAPÍTULO

4

¡Adelante con los estudios!

■ TERCER PASO Student Make-Up Assignments Checklist

Pupil's Edition, pp. 110–112

Study the expressions in the **Vocabulario** box on page 110: **Hacer planes para...**	☐ Do Activity 28, p. 110, as a writing activity. ☐ For additional practice, do Activity 7, p. 119 in **Más práctica gramatical**. ☐ For additional practice, do Activities 16–17, p. 44 in the **Cuaderno de actividades**. ☐ For additional practice, do Activity 18, p. 34 in the **Cuaderno de gramática**. ☐ For additional practice, do Activity 6, CD 1 in the **Interactive CD-ROM Tutor**.
Study the expressions in the **Así se dice** box on page 111: making plans. You should know how to make plans.	☐ Do Activity 30, p. 111 as a writing activity. ☐ For additional practice, do Activity 18, p. 45 in the **Cuaderno de actividades**.
Study the grammar presentation in the **Gramática** box on page 112: direct object pronouns.	☐ Do Activity 31, p. 112. ☐ Do Activity 32, p. 112, as a writing activity. ☐ Do Activity 33, p. 112, as a writing activity. Write a conversation. ☐ For additional practice, do Activity 8, p. 119 in **Más práctica gramatical**. ☐ For additional practice, do Activities 19–20, pp. 45–46 in the **Cuaderno de actividades**. ☐ For additional practice, do Activities 19–20, pp. 34–35 in the **Cuaderno de gramática**. ☐ For additional practice, do Activity 5, CD 1 in the **Interactive CD-ROM Tutor**.

CAPÍTULO 4

◼ TERCER PASO Self-Test

Can you make plans?	Complete the following dialogue.

TÚ	—¿...al cine conmigo?
TU COMPAÑERO	—No puedo; hoy no tengo tiempo.
TÚ	—Bueno, entonces, ¿...vamos mañana?
TÚ COMPAÑERO	—De acuerdo. ...a las seis.
TÚ	—... Hasta mañana.
TU COMPAÑERO	—Sí, ...mañana.

 For an **online self-test**, go to **go.hrw.com**.

WV3 Mexico–4

CAPÍTULO 5

¡Ponte en forma!

■ PRIMER PASO Student Make-Up Assignments Checklist

Pupil's Edition, pp. 133–137

Study the expressions in the **Vocabulario** box on page 133: **¿Qué deporte te gustaría practicar?**	☐ Do Activity 6, p. 133, as a writing activity. ☐ For additional practice, do Activity 3, p. 50 in the **Cuaderno de actividades.** ☐ For additional practice, do Activities 1–2, p. 36 in the **Cuaderno de gramática.**
Study the expressions in the **Así se dice** box on page 134: talking about staying fit and healthy. You should know how to talk about staying fit and healthy.	☐ Do Activity 8, p. 134, as a writing activity. ☐ Do Activity 9, p. 135. ☐ Do Activity 10, p. 135, as a writing activity.
Study the grammar presentation in the **Nota gramatical** box on page 134: **dormir.**	☐ For additional practice, do Activity 1, p. 150 in **Más práctica gramatical.** ☐ For additional practice, do Activity 5, p. 51 in the **Cuaderno de actividades.** ☐ For additional practice, do Activity 3, p. 37 in the **Cuaderno de gramática.**
Study the expressions in the **Vocabulario** box on page 135.	☐ Do Activity 11, p. 135. ☐ Do Activity 16, p. 137, as a writing activity. ☐ For additional practice, do Activity 2, p. 150 in **Más práctica gramatical.** ☐ For additional practice, do Activities 4, 6, pp. 50–51 in the **Cuaderno de actividades.** ☐ For additional practice, do Activities 4–5, pp. 37–38 in the **Cuaderno de gramática.** ☐ For additional practice, do Activity 1, CD 2 in the **Interactive CD-ROM Tutor.**
Study the grammar presentation in the **Gramática** box on page 136: preterite of **-er** and **-ir** verbs.	☐ Do Activity 12, p. 136, as a writing activity. ☐ Do Activity 13, p. 136. ☐ Do Activity 14, p. 137, as a writing activity. ☐ Do Activity 15, p. 137, as a writing activity. Write about yourself.

CAPÍTULO 5

☐ Do Activity 17, p. 137.

☐ For additional practice, do Activity 3, p. 151 in **Más práctica gramatical.**

☐ For additional practice, do Activity 7, p. 52 in the **Cuaderno de actividades.**

☐ For additional practice, do Activities 6–7, p. 38 in the **Cuaderno de gramática.**

☐ For additional practice, do Activity 2, CD 2 in the **Interactive CD-ROM Tutor.**

■ PRIMER PASO Self-Test

CAPÍTULO 6

Can you talk about staying fit and healthy?	How would you ask the following people how they stay in shape? Look at the pictures in Activity 1, on page 156, above the person's name. How would she or he answer?

Maribel

Carla

Pedro

Gustavo

Jimena

José

Say what the following people did during Health Week.

1. yo/ir al gimnasio

2. Fernando/correr cinco kilómetros

3. los profesores/dar un paseo en bicicleta

4. nosotros/inscribirse en una clase de remo

5. Laura/escalar una montaña

6. Luis y Norma/hacer ejercicios aeróbicos

7. tú/comer una dieta sana y balanceada

For an **online self-test**, go to **go.hrw.com.**

WV3 TEXAS-5

Holt Spanish 2 ¡Ven conmigo!, Chapter 5

CAPÍTULO 5 ¡Ponte en forma!

■ SEGUNDO PASO Student Make-Up Assignments Checklist

Pupil's Edition, pp. 138–141

Study the expressions in the **Así se dice** box on page 138: telling someone what to do and not to do. You should know how to tell someone what to do and not to do.	☐ For additional practice, do Activity 9, p. 53 in the **Cuaderno de actividades**. ☐ For additional practice, do Activity 4, CD 2 in the **Interactive CD-ROM Tutor**.
Study the expressions in the **Vocabulario** box on page 139.	☐ Do Activity 20, p. 139. ☐ For additional practice, do Activities 8, 10, pp. 53–54 in the **Cuaderno de actividades**. ☐ For additional practice, do Activities 10–11, p. 40 in the **Cuaderno de gramática**.
Study the grammar presentation in the **Gramática** box on page 139: informal commands.	☐ Do Activity 21, p. 140, as a writing activity. ☐ For additional practice, do Activity 4, p. 151 in **Más práctica gramatical**. ☐ For additional practice, do Activity 12, p. 55 in the **Cuaderno de actividades**. ☐ For additional practice, do Activity 12, p. 41 in the **Cuaderno de gramática**. ☐ For additional practice, do Activity 3, CD 2 in the **Interactive CD-ROM Tutor**.
Study the grammar presentation in the **Nota gramatical** box on page 140.	☐ Do Activity 22, p. 140, as a writing activity. ☐ For additional practice, do Activity 5, p. 152 in **Más práctica gramatical**.
Study the grammar presentation in the **Gramática** box on page 140: irregular informal commands.	☐ Do Activity 23, p. 141, as a writing activity. ☐ Do Activity 24, p. 141, as a writing activity. ☐ Do Activity 25, p. 141, as a writing activity. ☐ Do Activity 26, p. 141. ☐ For additional practice, do Activity 4, p. 151 in **Más práctica gramatical**. ☐ For additional practice, do Activity 11, p. 54 in the **Cuaderno de actividades**.

CAPÍTULO 5

☐ For additional practice, do Activities 13–14, p. 42 in the **Cuaderno de gramática.**

☐ For additional practice, do Activity 3, CD 2 in the **Interactive CD-ROM Tutor.**

◼ SEGUNDO PASO Self-Test

| Can you tell someone what to do and not to do? | How would you tell your friend to do the following things? |

Can you tell someone what to do and not to do?

How would you tell your friend to do the following things?

1. hacer ejercicio
2. practicar el ciclismo
3. ir al gimnasio
4. evitar el estrés
5. beber ocho vasos de agua
6. tener buenos hábitos

How would you tell your friend *not* to do the following things?

1. fumar
2. salir todas las noches
3. ser flojo/a
4. dormir sólo tres horas
5. comer grasas
6. llegar tarde

For an **online self-test**, go to **go.hrw.com.**

WV3 TEXAS-5

CAPÍTULO

5 ¡Ponte en forma!

■ TERCER PASO Student Make-Up Assignments Checklist

Pupil's Edition, pp. 143–146

Study the expressions in the **Así se dice** box on page 143: giving explanations. You should know how to give explanations.	☐ For additional practice, do Activity 13, p. 56 in the **Cuaderno de actividades.** ☐ For additional practice, do Activity 5, CD 2 in the **Interactive CD-ROM Tutor.**
Study the grammar presentation in the **Nota gramatical** box on page 144: **poder.**	☐ Do Activity 29, p. 144, as a writing activity. ☐ Do Activity 30, p. 144, as a writing activity. Write a possible conversation between two friends in which one asks the other what he or she was able to do over the weekend. ☐ For additional practice, do Activity 6, p. 144 in **Más práctica gramatical.** ☐ For additional practice, do Activity 14, p. 57 in the **Cuaderno de actividades.** ☐ For additional practice, do Activity 15, p. 43 in the **Cuaderno de gramática.**
Study the expressions in the **Vocabulario** box on page 145: parts of the body.	☐ Do Activity 31, p. 145, as a writing activity. ☐ Do Activity 32, p. 145, as a writing activity. Write a conversation between two friends. Use the clues from the exercise. ☐ For additional practice, do Activities 15–17, pp. 57–58 in the **Cuaderno de actividades.** ☐ For additional practice, do Activities 16–17, p. 43 in the **Cuaderno de gramática.** ☐ For additional practice, do Activity 6, CD 2 in the **Interactive CD-ROM Tutor.**
Study the expressions in the **Vocabulario** box on page 145: parts of the body.	☐ For additional practice, do Activity 18, p. 44 in the **Cuaderno de gramática.**
Study the grammar presentation in the **Nota gramatical** box on page 146.	☐ Do Activity 33, p. 146, as a writing activity. ☐ Do Activity 34, p. 146, as a writing activity. ☐ Do Activity 35, p. 146, as a writing activity.

CAPÍTULO 5

☐ For additional practice, do Activity 7, p. 153 in **Más práctica gramatical.**

☐ For additional practice, do Activity 19, p. 44 in the **Cuaderno de gramática.**

▓ TERCER PASO Self-Test

Can you give explanations?	Look at the drawings in Activity 5 of **A ver si puedo...** on page 156 in your textbook. What would each person give as an explanation for not playing soccer?

Mónica

Rubén

Víctor

Sandra

For an **online self-test**, go to **go.hrw.com**.

WV3 TEXAS-5

Holt Spanish 2 ¡Ven conmigo!, Chapter 5

CAPÍTULO 5

CAPÍTULO

6 De visita en la ciudad

■ PRIMER PASO Student Make-Up Assignments Checklist
Pupil's Edition, pp. 163-166

Study the expressions in the **Vocabulario** box on page 163.	☐ Do Activity 6, p. 163, as a writing activity. Allow yourself one minute to write as many items per category as possible. ☐ For additional practice, do Activity 1, p. 178 in **Más práctica gramatical**. ☐ For additional practice, do Activity 2, p. 62 in the **Cuaderno de actividades**. ☐ For additional practice, do Activities 1–2, p. 45 in the **Cuaderno de gramática**. ☐ For additional practice, do Activity 1, CD 2 in the **Interactive CD-ROM Tutor**.
Study the expressions in the **Así se dice** box on page 164: asking for and giving information. You should know how to ask for and give information.	☐ Do Activity 8, p. 165, as a writing activity. ☐ Do Activity 9, p. 165, as a writing activity. Write a possible conversation. ☐ For additional practice, do Activities 3–4, pp. 62–63 in the **Cuaderno de actividades**.
Study the grammar presentation in the **Nota gramatical** box on page 164: the verb **saber**.	☐ For additional practice, do Activity 2, p. 178 in **Más práctica gramatical**. ☐ For additional practice, do Activity 5, p. 63 in the **Cuaderno de actividades**. ☐ For additional practice, do Activities 3–5, p. 46 in the **Cuaderno de gramática**.
Study the grammar presentation in the **Gramática** box on page 165: **saber** vs. **conocer**.	☐ Do Activity 10, p. 166. ☐ Do Activity 11, p. 166, as a writing activity. ☐ Do Activity 12, p. 166, as a writing activity. ☐ Do Activity 13, p. 166. ☐ For additional practice, do Activity 3, p. 178 in **Más práctica gramatical**. ☐ For additional practice, do Activities 6–7, p. 64 in the **Cuaderno de actividades**. ☐ For additional practice, do Activities 6–7, p. 47 in the **Cuaderno de gramática**. ☐ For additional practice, do Activity 2, CD 2 in the **Interactive CD-ROM Tutor**.

CAPÍTULO 6

■ PRIMER PASO Self-Test

Can you ask for and give information?	How would you ask an older person the following things? How would you ask someone who is your own age? How would you answer if you weren't sure or had no idea . . . ? 1. what time it is 2. if he knows the waitperson 3. where to get off the bus 4. where the museum is 5. how much the tickets cost 6. if she knows the café Tacos Pacos Tell someone what your favorite restaurant is and explain why.

For an **online self-test**, go to **go.hrw.com**.

WV3 TEXAS-6

CAPÍTULO 6

Holt Spanish 2 ¡Ven conmigo!, Chapter 6

6 De visita en la ciudad

CAPÍTULO

■ SEGUNDO PASO Student Make-Up Assignments Checklist

Pupil's Edition, pp. 167–170

Study the expressions in the **Vocabulario** box on page 167.	☐ Do Activity 14, p. 167, as a writing activity. ☐ For additional practice, do Activities 8–9, p. 65 in the **Cuaderno de actividades.**
Study the expressions in the **Así se dice** box on page 168: relating a series of events. You should know how to relate a series of events.	☐ Do Activity 16, p. 148. ☐ For additional practice, do Activities 10–12, pp. 66–67 in the **Cuaderno de actividades.** ☐ For additional practice, do Activities 10, 12–13, pp. 49–50 in the **Cuaderno de gramática.** ☐ For additional practice, do Activity 3, CD 2 in the **Interactive CD-ROM Tutor.**
Study the expressions in the **Vocabulario** box on page 169.	☐ Do Activity 17, p. 169. ☐ Do Activity 18, p. 170, as a writing activity. Write descriptions that could serve as riddles for some of the words in the exercise. ☐ Do Activity 19, p. 170, as a writing activity. ☐ Do Activity 20, p. 170, as a writing activity. Write an ending to the story started in the exercise. ☐ Do Activity 21, p. 170. ☐ For additional practice, do Activity 6, p. 180 in **Más práctica gramatical.** ☐ For additional practice, do Activities 8–9, p. 48 in the **Cuaderno de gramática.**

CAPÍTULO 6

■ SEGUNDO PASO Self-Test

| Can you relate a series of events? | Say you went to the places pictured in Activity 3 of **A ver si puedo...** on page 184 in your textbook, and tell what you did there. Establish a sequence: first . . ., then . . . |

 For an **online self-test**, go to **go.hrw.com**.

WV3 TEXAS-6

CAPÍTULO 6

CAPÍTULO

6 De visita en la ciudad

■ TERCER PASO Student Make-Up Assignments Checklist

Pupil's Edition, pp. 172–175

Study the expressions in the **Así se dice** box on page 172: ordering in a restaurant. You should know how to order in a restaurant.	☐ Do Activity 23, p. 173, as a writing activity. ☐ For additional practice, do Activity 13, p. 68 in the **Cuaderno de actividades.** ☐ For additional practice, do Activity 5, CD 2 in the **Interactive CD-ROM Tutor.**
Study the expressions in the **Vocabulario** box on page 173.	☐ For additional practice, do Activity 14, p. 51 in the **Cuaderno de gramática.** ☐ For additional practice, do Activity 6, CD 2 in the **Interactive CD-ROM Tutor.**
Study the grammar presentation in the **Gramática** box on page 174: preterite forms of **pedir** and **servir.**	☐ Do Activity 25, p. 174, as a writing activity. ☐ For additional practice, do Activity 7, p. 181 in **Más práctica gramatical.** ☐ For additional practice, do Activity 14, p. 69 in the **Cuaderno de actividades.** ☐ For additional practice, do Activity 15, p. 51 in the **Cuaderno de gramática.** ☐ For additional practice, do Activity 4, CD 4 in the **Interactive CD-ROM Tutor.**
Study the grammar presentation in the **Nota gramatical** box on page 174: the verb **traer.**	☐ Do Activity 26, p. 174, as a writing activity. ☐ Do Activity 27, p. 175, as a writing activity. Write a conversation. ☐ Do Activity 28, p. 175. ☐ Do Activity 29, p. 175. ☐ For additional practice, do Activities 7–8, p. 181 in **Más práctica gramatical.** ☐ For additional practice, do Activities 15–16, pp. 69–70 in the **Cuaderno de actividades.** ☐ For additional practice, do Activities 16–18, 21, pp. 52–53 in the **Cuaderno de gramática.**

CAPÍTULO 6

■ TERCER PASO Self-Test

Can you order in a restaurant?	Say that these people asked for the following items.

1. Miguel—agua mineral
2. Lupe y Carla—la especialidad de la casa
3. nosotros—para el postre, flan
4. Jimena—¿?
5. tú—la cuenta

If you were the host or hostess at a dinner, how would you ask your guests the following? How might your guests respond?

1. if they know what they want to order
2. what they want to drink
3. what they would like for dessert
4. if they want anything else

 For an **online self-test**, go to **go.hrw.com**.

WV3 TEXAS-6

CAPÍTULO 6

¿Conoces bien tu pasado?

■ PRIMER PASO Student Make-Up Assignments Checklist

Pupil's Edition, pp. 195–199

Study the expressions in the **Así se dice** box on page 196: talking about what you used to do. You should know how to talk about what you used to do.	☐ For additional practice, do Activity 3, p. 74 in the **Cuaderno de actividades.**
Study the grammar presentation in the **Gramática** box on page 196: the imperfect tense.	☐ Do Activity 8, p. 196. ☐ Do Activity 9, p. 197, as a writing activity. ☐ Do Activity 10, p. 196, as a writing activity. ☐ For additional practice, do Activity 1, p. 212 in **Más práctica gramatical.** ☐ For additional practice, do Activities 4–5, p. 74 in the **Cuaderno de actividades.** ☐ For additional practice, do Activities 1–5, pp. 54–55 in the **Cuaderno de gramática.**
Study the grammar presentation in the **Nota gramatical** box on page 197: the verbs **ir** and **ver.**	☐ Do Activity 11, p. 197. ☐ For additional practice, do Activity 2, p. 197 in **Más práctica gramatical.** ☐ For additional practice, do Activity 6, p. 56 in the **Cuaderno de gramática.** ☐ For additional practice, do Activity 2, CD 2 in the **Interactive CD-ROM Tutor.**
Study the expressions in the **Vocabulario** box on page 198.	☐ Do Activity 12, p. 198, as a writing activity. ☐ For additional practice, do Activity 3, p. 213 in **Más práctica gramatical.** ☐ For additional practice, do Activity 7, p. 56 in the **Cuaderno de gramática.** ☐ For additional practice, do Activity 1, CD 2 in the **Interactive CD-ROM Tutor.**

CAPÍTULO 7

Study the expressions in the **Así se dice** box on page 198: saying what you used to like and dislike. You should know how to say what you used to like and dislike.

☐ Do Activity 14, p. 199, as a writing activity.

☐ Do Activity 15, p. 199, as a writing activity.

☐ Do Activity 16a, p. 199.

☐ For additional practice, do Activities 6–7, pp. 75–76 in the **Cuaderno de actividades**.

PRIMER PASO Self-Test

Can you talk about what you used to do?	Complete each of the following sentences, saying what you used to do when you were little.
	1. El primer día de vacaciones siempre...
	2. El día cuatro de julio, mi familia y yo generalmente
	3. Después de las clases, mis amistades y yo...
	4. Los sábados por la mañana, muchas veces yo...
	5. El día de mi cumpleaños, yo...
	6. Los días cuando llovía, a veces yo...
Can you say what you used to like and dislike?	Think back to what you liked and didn't like when you were little. How did you feel about the following things?
	1. las películas de ciencia ficción
	2. el helado de chocolate
	3. bañarte todas las noches
	4. ir al parque

 For an **online self-test**, go to **go.hrw.com**.

WV3 CARIBE-7

Holt Spanish 2 ¡Ven conmigo!, Chapter 7

CAPÍTULO

7 ¿Conoces bien tu pasado?

■ SEGUNDO PASO Student Make-Up Assignments Checklist

Pupil's Edition, pp. 201–205

Study the grammar presentation in the **Nota gramatical** box on page 201: **o>u, y>e** in conjunctions.	☐ For additional practice, do Activity 4, pp. 213–214 in **Más práctica gramatical.** ☐ For additional practice, do Activities 8–9, p. 57 in the **Cuaderno de gramática.**
Study the expressions in the **Así se dice** box on page 202: describing what people and things were like. You should know how to describe what people and things were like.	☐ For additional practice, do Activity 9, p. 78 in the **Cuaderno de actividades.**
Study the expressions in the **Vocabulario** box on page 202.	☐ Do Activity 19, p. 203, as a writing activity. ☐ For additional practice, do Activity 8, p. 77 in the **Cuaderno de actividades.** ☐ For additional practice, do Activities 12–13, p. 59 in the **Cuaderno de gramática.** ☐ For additional practice, do Activity 4, CD 2 in the **Interactive CD-ROM Tutor.**
Study the grammar presentation in the **Nota gramatical** box on page 203: the verb **ser.**	☐ Do Activity 20, p. 203, as a writing activity. ☐ Do Activity 21, p. 203, as a writing activity. ☐ Do Activity 22, p. 203, as a writing activity. ☐ For additional practice, do Activity 5, p. 214 in **Más práctica gramatical.** ☐ For additional practice, do Activity 10, p. 10 in the **Cuaderno de actividades.** ☐ For additional practice, do Activities 10–11, 19, pp. 58, 61 in the **Cuaderno de gramática.**
Study the expressions in the **Vocabulario** box on page 204.	☐ Do Activity 23, p. 204. ☐ For additional practice, do Activity 11, p. 79 in the **Cuaderno de actividades.** ☐ For additional practice, do Activities 14–15, p. 60 in the **Cuaderno de gramática.**

CAPÍTULO 7

Study the grammar presentation in the **Nota gramatical** box on page 204: the imperfect of **hay**.	☐ Do Activity 24, p. 204, as a writing activity. ☐ For additional practice, do Activity 6, p. 214 in **Más práctica gramatical**. ☐ For additional practice, do Activity 12, p. 79 in the **Cuaderno de actividades**. ☐ For additional practice, do Activities 17–18, p. 61 in the **Cuaderno de gramática**. ☐ For additional practice, do Activity 3, CD 2 in the **Interactive CD-ROM Tutor**.
Study the expressions in the **Vocabulario** box on page 204.	☐ Do Activity 26, p. 205, as a writing activity. ☐ Do Activity 27, p. 205, as a writing activity. ☐ Do Activity 28, p. 205, as a writing activity. ☐ For additional practice, do Activity 16, p. 81 in the **Cuaderno de actividades**. ☐ For additional practice, do Activity 16, p. 60 in the **Cuaderno de gramática**.

■ SEGUNDO PASO Self-Test

Can you describe what people and things were like?	How much do you remember from your childhood? Describe why you liked or didn't like the following people and places, giving as many details as you can. 1. tu cuarto 2. el centro comercial 3. tu escuela 4. tu casa 5. tu maestro/a de primer grado 6. el supermercado 7. un personaje de televisión 8. el niño o la niña vecino/a You and a new friend are looking at some old photos. Tell your friend what the people in the photos in Activity 4 of **A ver si puedo...** on page 218 in your textbook were like. Marco　　　　　Graciela Inés y Margarita　　Pablo y Pedro

For an **online self-test**, go to **go.hrw.com**.

WV3 CARIBE-7

　　　　Holt Spanish 2 ¡Ven conmigo!, Chapter 7

CAPÍTULO 7

7 ¿Conoces bien tu pasado?

■ TERCER PASO Student Make-Up Assignments Checklist
Pupil's Edition, pp. 206–208

Study the expressions in the Así se dice box on page 206: using comparisons to describe people. You should know how to use comparison to describe people.	☐ Do Activity 30, p. 207. ☐ For additional practice, do Activities 13, 15, pp. 80–81 in the **Cuaderno de actividades.**
Study the grammar presentation in the **Gramática** box on page 207: comparisons of equality.	☐ Do Activity 31, p. 207, as a writing activity. ☐ Do Activity 32, p. 208, as a writing activity. ☐ Do Activity 33, p. 208, as a writing activity. ☐ Do Activity 34, p. 208, as a writing activity. ☐ For additional practice, do Activities 7–8, p. 215 in **Más práctica gramatical.** ☐ For additional practice, do Activities 14,17, pp. 80, 82 in the **Cuaderno de actividades.** ☐ For additional practice, do Activities 20–23, pp. 62–63 in the **Cuaderno de gramática.** ☐ For additional practice, do Activity 6, CD 2 in the **Interactive CD-ROM Tutor.**

CAPÍTULO 7

■ TERCER PASO Self-Test

Can you use comparisons to describe people?	Look at the drawings in Activity 4 of **A ver si puedo...** on page 218 in your textbook, and compare the following people.

1. Pedro y Pablo
2. Graciela e Inés
3. Marco y Margarita
4. Inés y Margarita
5. Pedro y Marco
6. Pablo y Graciela

 For an **online self-test**, go to **go.hrw.com**.

WV3 CARIBE-7

CAPÍTULO 8

Diversiones

■ PRIMER PASO Student Make-Up Assignments Checklist

Pupil's Edition, pp. 225–228

Study the expressions in the **Así se dice** box on page 225: describing a past event. You should know how to describe a past event.	☐ For additional practice, do Activity 3, p. 86 in the **Cuaderno de actividades**. ☐ For additional practice, do Activity 1, CD 2 in the **Interactive CD-ROM Tutor**.
Study the grammar presentation in the **Nota gramatical** box on page 225.	☐ Do Activity 8, p. 225, as a writing activity. ☐ Do Activity 9, p. 226, as a writing activity. ☐ For additional practice, do Activity 1, p. 240 in **Más práctica gramatical**. ☐ For additional practice, do Activities 4, 6, pp. 86, 88 in the **Cuaderno de actividades**. ☐ For additional practice, do Activities 1–2, p. 64 in the **Cuaderno de gramática**.
Study the expressions in the **Vocabulario** box on page 226: **en el zoológico...**	☐ Do Activity 10, p. 227. ☐ Do Activity 11, p. 227, as a writing activity. ☐ For additional practice, do Activity 5, p. 87 in the **Cuaderno de actividades**. ☐ For additional practice, do Activities 3–4, p. 65 in the **Cuaderno de gramática**. ☐ For additional practice, do Activity 2, CD 2 in the **Interactive CD-ROM Tutor**.
Study the **Vocabulario** on page 237.	☐ For additional practice, do Activity 7, p. 88 in the **Cuaderno de actividades**. ☐ For additional practice, do Activities 5–6, p. 63 in the **Cuaderno de gramática**. ☐ For additional practice, do Activity 2, CD 2 in the **Interactive CD-ROM Tutor**.
Study the grammar presentation in the **Gramática** box on page 227: superlatives.	☐ Do Activity 12, p. 227, as a writing activity. ☐ Do Activity 13, p. 228, as a writing activity. ☐ Do Activity 14, p. 228, as a writing activity. ☐ Do Activity 15, p. 228, as a writing activity.

CAPÍTULO 8

☐ Do Activity 16, p. 228.

☐ For additional practice, do Activity 2, p. 240 in **Más práctica gramatical.**

☐ For additional practice, do Activity 7, p. 88 in the **Cuaderno de actividades.**

☐ For additional practice, do Activities 5–7, pp. 65–66 in the **Cuaderno de gramática.**

☐ For additional practice, do Activity 3, CD 2 in the **Interactive CD-ROM Tutor.**

■ PRIMER PASO Self-Test

CAPÍTULO 8

| Can you describe a past event? | Using the following adjectives and the ending -**ísimo,** describe various events of last weekend to a friend. |

aburrido

corto

bueno

interesante

malo

alegre

What did you see at the following places? Use the clues to describe what you saw using superlatives.

1. cine/una película mala

2. parque de atracciones/una montañarusa grande

3. zoológico/un mono cómico

4. estadio/un partido emocionante

5. concierto/un cantante bueno

 For an **online self-test**, go to **go.hrw.com.**

WV3 CARIBE-7

CAPÍTULO

Diversiones

■ SEGUNDO PASO Student Make-Up Assignments Checklist

Pupil's Edition, pp. 229–232

Study the expressions in the **Vocabulario** box on page 229: **hacer un mandado.**	☐ Do Activity 17, p. 229, as a writing activity. ☐ For additional practice, do Activity 3, p. 241 in **Más práctica gramatical.** ☐ For additional practice, do Activities 8–9, p. 67 in the **Cuaderno de gramática.** ☐ For additional practice, do Activity 5, CD 2 in the **Interactive CD-ROM Tutor.**
Study the expressions in the **Así se dice** box on page 230: saying why you couldn't do something. You should know how to say why you couldn't do something.	☐ Do Activity 19, p. 230, as a writing activity. ☐ Do Activity 20, p. 231, as a writing activity. ☐ Do Activity 21, p. 231, as a writing activity. ☐ Do Activity 22, p. 231, as a writing activity. ☐ For additional practice, do Activities 8–10, pp. 89–91 in the **Cuaderno de actividades.**
Study the grammar presentation in the **Nota gramatical** box on page 231: verbs followed by a preposition.	☐ Do Activity 23, p. 232. ☐ Do Activity 24, p. 232, as a writing activity. ☐ Do Activity 25, p. 232. ☐ For additional practice, do Activity 4, p. 241 in **Más práctica gramatical.** ☐ For additional practice, do Activities 10–11, p. 68 in the **Cuaderno de gramática.**
Study the grammar presentation in the **Nota gramatical** box on page 231: **mientras** and the imperfect tense.	☐ Do Activity 23, p. 232, as a writing activity. ☐ For additional practice, do Activity 5, p. 242 in **Más práctica gramatical.** ☐ For additional practice, do Activity 11, p. 91 in the **Cuaderno de actividades.** ☐ For additional practice, do Activities 12–13, p. 69 in the **Cuaderno de gramática.** ☐ For additional practice, do Activity 4, CD 2 in the **Interactive CD-ROM Tutor.**

CAPÍTULO 8

■ SEGUNDO PASO Self-Test

| Can you say why you couldn't do something? | Look at the pictures in Activity 3 of **A ver si puedo...** on page 246 in your textbook. How would you tell a friend that you wanted or planned to do those activities but couldn't because you had errands to run?

1. ir al parque de atracciones

2. ver el estreno

3. reunirse con amigos

4. ir al partido de béisbol

Look at the activities and pictures in Activity 3 of **A ver si puedo...** on page 246 in your textbook. Use **mientras** and the imperfect tense to say what errands you were running while your friends were having fun. |

For an **online self-test,** go to **go.hrw.com.**

WV3 CARIBE-8

Holt Spanish 2 ¡Ven conmigo!, Chapter 8

CAPÍTULO 8

CAPÍTULO

Nombre _____ Clase _____ Fecha _____

8 Diversiones

■ TERCER PASO Student Make-Up Assignments Checklist

Pupil's Edition, pp. 234–237

Study the expressions in the **Así se dice** box on page 235: reporting what someone said. You should know how to report what someone said.	☐ For additional practice, do Activities 12, 15, p. 92 in the **Cuaderno de actividades.**
Study the expressions in the **Vocabulario** box on page 235: **en el festival...**	☐ Do Activity 8, p. 235, as a writing activity. ☐ For additional practice, do Activity 1, p. 240 in **Más práctica gramatical.** ☐ For additional practice, do Activity 13, p. 92 in the **Cuaderno de actividades.** ☐ For additional practice, do Activities 14–15, p. 70 in the **Cuaderno de gramática.**
Study the grammar presentation in the **Gramática** box on page 236: **decir** in the preterite.	☐ Do Activity 29, p. 236, as a writing activity. ☐ Do Activity 30, p. 236, as a writing activity. ☐ Do Activity 31, p. 237, as a writing activity. ☐ Do Activity 32, p. 237, as a writing activity. ☐ Do Activity 33, p. 237. ☐ For additional practice, do Activities 6–7, pp. 242–243 in **Más práctica gramatical.** ☐ For additional practice, do Activities 14, 16, pp. 93–94 in the **Cuaderno de actividades.** ☐ For additional practice, do Activities 16–17, p. 71 in the **Cuaderno de gramática.** ☐ For additional practice, do Activity 6, CD 2 in the **Interactive CD-ROM Tutor.**

CAPÍTULO 8

◼ TERCER PASO Self-Test

Can you report what someone said?	How would you report what the following people said?

1. ROGELIO: Estoy casi muerto.

2. NORMA Y LUIS: Nosotros también.

3. LUIS: ¡Ponce es la ciudad más bonita de Puerto Rico!

4. ROGELIO: ¡Tengo hambre!

5. NORMA: Vamos a comer en el café de tío Martín.

 For an **online self-test,** go to **go.hrw.com.**

WV3 CARIBE-8

CAPÍTULO 8

CAPÍTULO

9 ¡Día de mercado!

■ PRIMER PASO Student Make-Up Assignments Checklist

Pupil's Edition, pp. 257–261

Study the expressions in the **Así se dice** box on page 258: asking for and giving directions. You should know how to ask for and give directions.	☐ For additional practice, do Activity 2, CD 3 in the **Interactive CD-ROM Tutor.**
Study the expressions in the **Vocabulario** box on page 258.	☐ Do Activity 8, p. 259, as a writing activity. ☐ Do Activity 9, p. 259. ☐ Do Activity 10, p. 259, as a writing activity. ☐ For additional practice, do Activity 1, p. 274 in **Más práctica gramatical.** ☐ For additional practice, do Activities 3–6, pp. 98–100 in the **Cuaderno de actividades.** ☐ For additional practice, do Activities 1–2, p. 72 in the **Cuaderno de gramática.** ☐ For additional practice, do Activity 1, CD 3 in the **Interactive CD-ROM Tutor.**
Study the grammar presentation in the **Gramática** box on page 260: formal commands (singular and plural).	☐ Do Activity 11, p. 260, as a writing activity. ☐ Do Activity 12, p. 261, as a writing activity. ☐ Do Activity 14, p. 261. ☐ For additional practice, do Activities 2-3, p. 275 in **Más práctica gramatical.** ☐ For additional practice, do Activity 7, p. 100 in the **Cuaderno de actividades.** ☐ For additional practice, do Activities 3–7, pp. 73–75 in the **Cuaderno de gramática.** ☐ For additional practice, do Activity 3, CD 3 in the **Interactive CD-ROM Tutor.**

CAPÍTULO 9

▨ PRIMER PASO Self-Test

Can you ask for and give directions?	How would you give directions to someone who wanted to go to the following places from your school?
	1. a un cine
	2. a tu restaurante favorito
	3. a un supermercado
	4. a una tienda de ropa

 For an **online self-test**, go to **go.hrw.com**.

WV3 ANDES-9

CAPÍTULO 9

CAPÍTULO

9 ¡Día de mercado!

■ SEGUNDO PASO Student Make-Up Assignments Checklist

Pupil's Edition, pp. 263–266

Study the expressions in the **Vocabulario** box on page 263: **en la tienda...**	☐ Do Activity 15, p. 263.
	☐ For additional practice, do Activity 8, p. 101 in the **Cuaderno de actividades.**
	☐ For additional practice, do Activities 8–10, p. 76 in the **Cuaderno de gramática.**
	☐ For additional practice, do Activity 4, CD 3 in the **Interactive CD-ROM Tutor.**
Study the expressions in the **Así se dice** box on page 264: asking for help in a store. You should know how to ask for help in a store.	☐ Do Activity 17, p. 264, as a writing activity.
	☐ Do Activity 18, p. 265, as a writing activity.
	☐ For additional practice, do Activity 9, p. 101 in the **Cuaderno de actividades.**
Study the expressions in the **Así se dice** box on page 265: talking about how clothes look and fit. You should know how to talk about how clothes look and fit.	☐ Do Activity 20, p. 266, as a writing activity.
	☐ Do Activity 21, p. 266, as a writing activity.
	☐ Do Activity 22, p. 266.
	☐ For additional practice, do Activity 4, p. 276 in **Más práctica gramatical.**
	☐ For additional practice, do Activities 10, 12, 19, pp. 102–103, 108 in the **Cuaderno de actividades.**
	☐ For additional practice, do Activity 5, CD 3 in the **Interactive CD-ROM Tutor.**

CAPÍTULO 9

▩ SEGUNDO PASO Self-Test

Can you ask for help in a store?	What would you say to the sales clerk in the following situations?
	1. Piensas comprarle una blusa a tu hermana. A ella le queda muy bien el verde.
	2. Estás de compras y quieres probarte un par de pantalones.
	3. El dependiente te pregunta qué talla usas.
	4. Necesitas hacerle una pregunta a la dependiente, pero parece estar ocupada en este momento.
	5. Perdiste tu chaqueta. El dependiente te pregunta de qué estilo y color quieres la nueva y también qué talla usas.
Can you talk about how clothes look and fit?	Ricardo and Carolina are trying on new clothes. Use the photos in Activity 3 of **A ver si puedo...** on page 280 in your textbook to describe how they look, and comment on the sizes.
	Your best friend wants to know how he or she looks in these clothes. Use comparisons to give your opinion.
	1. el sombrero rojo/intelectual
	2. la camisa blanca/elegante
	3. los bluejeans/cómodo
	4. los zapatos negros/alto
	5. la camiseta de rayas/de moda
	6. el pantalón gris/delgado

For an **online self-test**, go to **go.hrw.com**.

WV3 ANDES-9

CAPÍTULO 9

CAPÍTULO 9 ¡Día de mercado!

■ TERCER PASO Student Make-Up Assignments Checklist

Pupil's Edition, pp. 268–271

Study the expressions in the **Así se dice** box on page 269: bargaining in a market. You should know how to bargain in a market.	☐ For additional practice, do Activities 13–14, 16, pp. 104–106 in the **Cuaderno de actividades.** ☐ For additional practice, do Activity 6, CD 3 in the **Interactive CD-ROM Tutor.**
Study the expressions in the **Vocabulario** box on page 269.	☐ Do Activity 25, p. 269. ☐ Do Activity 27, p. 270, as a writing activity. ☐ Do Activity 28, p. 270, as a writing activity. ☐ Do Activity 29, p. 271, as a writing activity. ☐ Do Activity 30, p. 271. ☐ For additional practice, do Activity 6, p. 277 in **Más práctica gramatical.** ☐ For additional practice, do Activity 15, p. 105 in the **Cuaderno de actividades.** ☐ For additional practice, do Activities 12–13, pp. 78–79 in the **Cuaderno de gramática.**

CAPÍTULO 9

■ TERCER PASO Self-Test

Can you bargain in a market?	If you were trying to buy a hat at an open-air market, how would you complete the following dialogue?

<table>
<tr><td>TÚ</td><td>...</td></tr>
<tr><td>VENDEDOR</td><td>Este sombrero aquí cuesta 25 dólares.</td></tr>
<tr><td>TÚ</td><td>...</td></tr>
<tr><td>VENDEDOR</td><td>Bueno, a Ud. se lo regalo por veinte.</td></tr>
<tr><td>TÚ</td><td>...</td></tr>
<tr><td>VENDEDOR</td><td>Se lo puedo dar por 18 dólares pero es mi última oferta.</td></tr>
<tr><td>TÚ</td><td>...</td></tr>
</table>

For an **online self-test**, go to **go.hrw.com**.

WV3 ANDES-9

CAPÍTULO 9

Holt Spanish 2 ¡Ven conmigo!, Chapter 9

CAPÍTULO 10 ¡Cuéntame!

■ PRIMER PASO Student Make-Up Assignments Checklist

Pupil's Edition, pp. 288–292

Study the expressions in the **Así se dice** box on page 289: setting the scene for a story. You should know how to set a scene for a story.	☐ For additional practice, do Activities 3–4, pp. 110–111 in the **Cuaderno de actividades.**
Study the expressions in the **Vocabulario** box on page 289.	☐ Do Activity 8, p. 289. ☐ For additional practice, do Activity 1, p. 304 in **Más práctica gramatical.** ☐ For additional practice, do Activities 1–2, p. 80 in the **Cuaderno de gramática.**
Study the grammar presentation in the **Gramática** box on page 290: preterite and imperfect contrasted.	☐ Do Activity 9, p. 290, as a writing activity. ☐ Do Activity 10, p. 290. ☐ For additional practice, do Activities 2–3, p. 112 in **Más práctica gramatical.** ☐ For additional practice, do Activities 5–6, p. 112 in the **Cuaderno de actividades.** ☐ For additional practice, do Activities 4–7, pp. 81–82 in the **Cuaderno de gramática.** ☐ For additional practice, do Activity 2, CD 3 in the **Interactive CD-ROM Tutor.**
Study the expressions in the **Vocabulario** box on page 291.	☐ Do Activity 11, p. 291, as a writing activity. ☐ Do Activity 12, p. 291, as a writing activity. ☐ Do Activity 13, p. 292. ☐ For additional practice, do Activity 8, p. 83 in the **Cuaderno de gramatica.** ☐ For additional practice, do Activity 1, CD 3 in the **Interactive CD-ROM Tutor.**
Study the grammar presentation in the **Nota gramatical** box on page 291.	☐ For additional practice, do Activity 3, p. 305 in **Más práctica gramatical.** ☐ For additional practice, do Activity 9, p. 83 in the **Cuaderno de gramática.** ☐ For additional practice, do Activity 2, CD 3 in the **Interactive CD-ROM Tutor.**

CAPÍTULO 10

▨ PRIMER PASO Self-Test

Can you set the scene for a story?	Look at the pictures in Activity 1 of **A ver si puedo...** page on 310 in your textbook and combine them to set the scene for a story.

For an **online self-test,** go to **go.hrw.com**.

WV3 ANDES-10

10 ¡Cuéntame!

■ SEGUNDO PASO Student Make-Up Assignments Checklist

Pupil's Edition, pp. 294–297

Study the expressions in the **Así se dice** box on page 295: continuing and ending a story. You should know how to continue and end story.	☐ For additional practice, do Activities 7–8, p. 113 in the **Cuaderno de actividades.** ☐ For additional practice, do Activity 4, CD 3 in the **Interactive CD-ROM Tutor.**
Study the expressions in the **Vocabulario** box on page 295: **ciencia ficción y cuentos de hadas.**	☐ Do Activity 16, p. 295, as a writing activity. ☐ For additional practice, do Activity 4, p. 306 in **Más práctica gramatical.** ☐ For additional practice, do Activity 10, p. 114 in the **Cuaderno de actividades.** ☐ For additional practice, do Activities 10–11, p. 84 in the **Cuaderno de gramática.** ☐ For additional practice, do Activity 5, CD 3 in the **Interactive CD-ROM Tutor.**
Study the grammar presentation in the **Gramática** box on page 296: preterite and imperfect to tell a story.	☐ Do Activity 17, p. 296, as a writing activity. ☐ Do Activity 18, p. 296, as a writing activity. ☐ Do Activity 19, p. 297, as a writing activity. ☐ Do Activity 20, p. 297. ☐ For additional practice, do Activity 5, p. 306 in **Más práctica gramatical.** ☐ For additional practice, do Activities 9, 11–12, pp. 114–115 in the **Cuaderno de actividades.** ☐ For additional practice, do Activities 12–15, pp. 85–86 in the **Cuaderno de gramática.** ☐ For additional practice, do Activity 3, CD 3 in the **Interactive CD-ROM Tutor.**

CAPÍTULO 10

■ SEGUNDO PASO Self-Test

Can you continue and end a story?	Continue the story from Activity 1of **A ver si puedo...** on page 310 in your textbook. Use some of the following words.
	la estrella
	la galaxia
	la nave espacial
	el planeta
	el OVNI
	de repente
	entonces
	Al final

For an **online self-test**, go to **go.hrw.com**.

WV3 ANDES-10

CAPÍTULO 10
¡Cuéntame!

▓ TERCER PASO Student Make-Up Assignments Checklist

Pupil's Edition, pp. 298–301

Study the expressions in the **Vocabulario** box on page 298.	☐ Do Activity 21, p. 298. ☐ For additional practice, do Activity 6, p. 307 in **Más práctica gramatical.** ☐ For additional practice, do Activities 13–14, pp. 116–117 in the **Cuaderno de actividades.** ☐ For additional practice, do Activities 16–17, p. 87 in the **Cuaderno de gramática.**
Study the expressions in the **Así se dice** box on page 299: talking about the latest news. You should know how to talk about the latest news.	☐ Do Activity 22, p. 299, as a writing activity. ☐ Do Activity 23, p. 299, as a writing activity. ☐ For additional practice, do Activities 15–16, pp. 117–118 in the **Cuaderno de actividades.** ☐ For additional practice, do Activity 19, p. 88 in the **Cuaderno de gramática.**
Study the expressions in the **Así se dice** box on page 300: reacting to news. You should know how to react to news.	☐ Do Activity 25, p. 300, as a writing activity. ☐ For additional practice, do Activity 17, p. 118 in the **Cuaderno de actividades.** ☐ For additional practice, do Activity 6, CD 3 in the **Interactive CD-ROM Tutor.**
Study the grammar presentation in the **Nota gramatical** box on page 300: the preterite of the verb **tener.**	☐ Do Activity 26, p. 300, as a writing activity. ☐ Do Activity 27, p. 301, as a writing activity. ☐ Do Activity 28, p. 301, as a writing activity. ☐ Do Activity 29, p. 301. ☐ For additional practice, do Activities 6–7, p. 307 in **Más práctica gramatical.** ☐ For additional practice, do Activity 18, p. 88 in the **Cuaderno de gramática.**

CAPÍTULO 10

■ TERCER PASO Self-Test

Can you talk about the latest news?	How would you tell someone about the following? How might that person respond?
	1. un amigo que bailó toda la noche
	2. una estrella de cine famosa que conociste
	3. unos amigos que se pelearon
	4. un concierto de música
Can you react to news?	React to the following news flashes.
	1. Descubren vida en otro planeta.
	2. Tus mejores amigos rompieron.
	3. No hay clases el viernes.
	4. Sacaste A+ en el examen de español.

For an **online self-test,** go to **go.hrw.com.**

WV3 ANDES-1

CAPÍTULO 11 Nuestro medio ambiente

■ PRIMER PASO Student Make-Up Assignments Checklist

Pupil's Edition, pp. 321–324

Study the expressions in the **Vocabulario** box on page 321: **los problemas del medio ambiente.**	☐ Do Activity 6, p. 321, as a writing activity. ☐ For additional practice, do Activities 3–4, pp. 122–123 in the **Cuaderno de actividades.** ☐ For additional practice, do Activities 1–2, p. 89 in the **Cuaderno de gramática.**
Study the expressions in the **Así se dice** box on page 322: describing a problem. You should know how to describe a problem.	☐ For additional practice, do Activity 5, p. 123 in the **Cuaderno de actividades.**
Study the grammar presentation in the **Nota gramatical** box on page 291: negative words.	☐ Do Activity 8, p. 322, as a writing activity. ☐ Do Activity 9, p. 322, as a writing activity. ☐ For additional practice, do Activity 2, p. 338 in **Más práctica gramatical.** ☐ For additional practice, do Activity 6, p. 124 in the **Cuaderno de actividades.** ☐ For additional practice, do Activities 3–5, pp. 90–91 in the **Cuaderno de gramática.** ☐ For additional practice, do Activity 2, CD 3 in the **Interactive CD-ROM Tutor.**
Study the expressions in the **Vocabulario** box on page 323: **la naturaleza.**	☐ Do Activity 10, p. 323. ☐ Do Activity 11, p. 323, as a writing activity. ☐ Do Activity 12, p. 324, as a writing activity. ☐ Do Activity 13, p. 324, as a writing activity. ☐ Do Activity 14, p. 324, as a writing activity. ☐ For additional practice, do Activities 7–8, pp. 124–125 in the **Cuaderno de actividades.** ☐ For additional practice, do Activities 6–7, p. 91 in the **Cuaderno de gramática.** ☐ For additional practice, do Activity 1, CD 3 in the **Interactive CD-ROM Tutor.**

CAPÍTULO 11

■ PRIMER PASO Self-Test

Can you describe a problem?

Can you identify and describe three environmental or ecological problems from this list that
are affecting your city, state, or region?

1. la basura
2. el smog
3. la contaminación del agua
4. el ruido
5. el desperdicio de recursos naturales
6. el uso de muchas químicas

For an **online self-test**, go to **go.hrw.com**.

WV3 CALIFORNIA-11

CAPÍTULO 11

Nuestro medio ambiente

■ SEGUNDO PASO Student Make-Up Assignments Checklist

Pupil's Edition, pp. 326–329

Study the expressions in the **Así se dice** box on page 328: talking about consequences. You should know how to talk about consequences.	☐ Do Activity 18, p. 328, as a writing activity. ☐ Do Activity 19, p. 328. ☐ For additional practice, do Activities 9–10, pp. 125–126 in the **Cuaderno de actividades.** ☐ For additional practice, do Activity 8, p. 92 in the **Cuaderno de gramática.** ☐ For additional practice, do Activity 4, CD 3 in the **Interactive CD-ROM Tutor.**
Study the expressions in the **Así se dice** box on page 329: expressing agreement and disagreement. You should know how to express agreement and disagreement.	☐ Do Activity 21, p. 329, as a writing activity. ☐ Do Activity 22, p. 329, as a writing activity. ☐ For additional practice, do Activity 5, p. 340 in **Más práctica gramatical.** ☐ For additional practice, do Activities 11–12, pp. 126–127 in the **Cuaderno de actividades.** ☐ For additional practice, do Activities 9–11, pp. 92–93 in the **Cuaderno de gramática.** ☐ For additional practice, do Activity 3, CD 3 in the **Interactive CD-ROM Tutor.**

■ SEGUNDO PASO Self-Test

C A P Í T U L O   1 1

Can you talk about consequences?	How would you tell the Secretary General of the United States what some of the consequences of the following situations might be?
	1. Si no cuidamos las selvas tropicales...
	2. Si desperdiciamos los recursos naturales...
	3. Si usamos muchas químicas...
	4. Si destruimos la capa de ozono...
	5. Si no protegemos los animales en peligro de extinción...
Can you express agreement and disagreement?	How would you tell someone whether or not you agree or disagree with the following statements?
	1. El gobierno nunca hace nada. Por eso el sistema no funciona.
	2. Nos toca a todos hacer algo para mantener limpia la ciudad.
	3. La destrucción de las selvas tropicales no es un problema muy grave.
	4. Los problemas del medio ambiente sólo afectan a las personas que viven en las ciudades grandes .
	5. Si queremos mejorar la situación, tenemos que comenzar a cambiar nuestro estilo de vida.

 For an **online self-test**, go to **go.hrw.com**.

WV3 CALIFORNIA-11

CAPÍTULO 11

Nuestro medio ambiente

■ TERCER PASO Student Make-Up Assignments Checklist

Pupil's Edition, pp. 331–335

<table>
<tr>
<td>Study the expressions in the Así se dice box on page 332: talking about obligations and solutions. You should know how to talk about obligations and solutions.</td>
<td>☐ Do Activity 26, p. 332, as a writing activity.
☐ For additional practice, do Activities 13–14, p. 128 in the Cuaderno de actividades.</td>
</tr>
<tr>
<td>Study the expressions in the Vocabularios box on page 333: tú puedes...</td>
<td>☐ For additional practice, do Activities 15–16, p. 129 in the Cuaderno de actividades.
☐ For additional practice, do Activities 14–15, p. 95 in the Cuaderno de gramática.
☐ For additional practice, do Activity 6, CD 3 in the Interactive CD-ROM Tutor.</td>
</tr>
<tr>
<td>Study the grammar presentation in the Nota gramatical box on page 333: the word si.</td>
<td>☐ Do Activity 27, p. 333.
☐ Do Activity 28, p. 333, as a writing activity.
☐ For additional practice, do Activity 6, p. 340 in the section Más práctica gramatical.
☐ For additional practice, do Activity 17, p. 130 in the Cuaderno de actividades.
☐ For additional practice, do Activities 16–17, pp. 95–96 in the Cuaderno de gramática.</td>
</tr>
<tr>
<td>Study the grammar presentation in the Gramática box on page 334: nosotros commands.</td>
<td>☐ Do Activity 29, p. 334.
☐ Do Activity 30, p. 335, as a writing activity.
☐ Do Activity 31, p. 335, as a writing activity.
☐ For additional practice, do Activity 7, p. 341 in Más práctica gramatical.
☐ For additional practice, do Activity 18, p. 130 in the Cuaderno de actividades.
☐ For additional practice, do Activities 18–20, pp. 96–97 in the Cuaderno de gramática.
☐ For additional practice, do Activity 5, CD 3 in the Interactive CD-ROM Tutor.</td>
</tr>
</table>

CAPÍTULO 11

■ TERCER PASO Self-Test

Can you talk about obligations and solutions?	Look at the drawings in Activity 4 on the **A ver si puedo...** on page 344 in your textbook. How would you tell your friends about some creative ways to solve the problems in the drawings?

Under what conditions would the following situations take place?

1. Las grandes ciudades no van a tener problemas con el smog...

2. Las selvas tropicales ya no van a estar en peligro...

3. Ya no va a haber contaminación en las playas...

4. Las calles no van a estar sucias...

5. Nuestros hijos van a vivir mejor...

For an **online self-test**, go to **go.hrw.com**.

WV3 CALIFORNIA-11

12 Veranos pasados, veranos por venir

■ PRIMER PASO Student Make-Up Assignments Checklist

Pupil's Edition, pp. 351–354

Study the expressions in the **Vocabulario** box on page 351: writing letters.	☐ For additional practice, do Activity 2, p. 134 in the **Cuaderno de actividades.**
	☐ For additional practice, do Activities 1–3, pp. 98–99 in the **Cuaderno de gramática.**
Study the expressions in the **Así se dice** box on page 351: exchanging the latest news. You should know how to exchange the latest news.	☐ Do Activity 6, p. 351.
	☐ Do Activity 7, p. 351.
	☐ For additional practice, do Activities 4–5, p. 135 in the **Cuaderno de actividades.**
	☐ For additional practice, do Activity 1, CD 3 in the **Interactive CD-ROM Tutor.**
Study the expressions in the **Así se dice** box on page 352: talking about where you went and what you did. You should know how to talk about where you went and what you did.	☐ For additional practice, do Activity 3, CD 3 in the **Interactive CD-ROM Tutor.**
Study the expressions in the **Vocabulario** box on page 352.	☐ Do Activity 9, p. 353, as a writing activity.
	☐ Do Activity 10, p. 353.
	☐ For additional practice, do Activity 2–3, pp. 364–365 in **Más práctica gramatical.**
	☐ For additional practice, do Activity 3, p. 134 in the **Cuaderno de actividades.**
	☐ For additional practice, do Activities 4–5, p. 99 in the **Cuaderno de gramática.**
	☐ For additional practice, do Activity 2, CD 3 in the **Interactive CD-ROM Tutor.**
Study the expressions in the **Así se dice** box on page 353: telling when something happened. You should know how to tell something happened.	☐ Do Activity 12, p. 353.
	☐ Do Activity 13, p. 354, as a writing activity.
	☐ Do Activity 14, p. 354, as a writing activity.
	☐ Do Activity 15, p. 354, as a writing activity.
	☐ For additional practice, do Activity 6, p. 136 in the **Cuaderno de actividades.**

■ PRIMER PASO Self-Test

Can you exchange the latest news?	If you were writing a personal letter, how would you . . . ?
	1. greet your friend
	2. ask for some news about him or her
	3. tell your friend the latest news
	4. send greetings to your friend's family
	5. close your letter
Can you talk about where you went and what you did?	Write a paragraph about where you went on your last vacation and what you did there. If you prefer, describe an imaginary vacation.
Can you tell when something happened?	Look at the calendar in Activity 3 of **A ver si puedo...** on page 370 in your textbook. Imagine that you attended a Mexican Day of the Dead celebration last year. Tell your friend about something that happened at the following times:
	1. el 1 de noviembre
	2. al día siguiente
	3. el día anterior
	4. dos días después del 2
	5. la semana entera

 For an **online self-test**, go to **go.hrw.com**.

WV3 CALIFORNIA-12

CAPÍTULO 12 — Veranos pasados, veranos por venir

■ SEGUNDO PASO Student Make-Up Assignments Checklist

Pupil's Edition, pp. 356–358

Study the expressions in the **Así se dice** box on page 356: saying how you feel about people. You should know how to say how you feel about people.	☐ Do Activity 18, p. 357, as a writing activity. ☐ Do Activity 19, p. 357. ☐ For additional practice, do Activity 5, p. 366 in **Más práctica gramatical**. ☐ For additional practice, do Activities 7–10, pp. 137–139 in the **Cuaderno de actividades**.
Study the expressions in the **Así se dice** box on page 358: describing places. You should know how to describe places.	☐ Do Activity 21, p. 358, as a writing activity. ☐ Do Activity 22, p. 358, as a writing activity. ☐ Do Activity 23, p. 358. For additional practice, do Activity 6, p. 366 in **Más práctica gramatical**. ☐ For additional practice, do Activity 11, p. 139 in the **Cuaderno de actividades**. ☐ For additional practice, do Activity 4, CD 3 in the **Interactive CD-ROM Tutor**.

CAPÍTULO 12

Nombre _____ Clase _____ Fecha _____

■ SEGUNDO PASO Self-Test

Can you say how you feel about people?	Your school paper is putting together a survey on the students' favorite and least favorite people. Say how you feel about . . . 1. your best friend 2. a member of a TV family 3. your next-door neighbors 4. your favorite band 5. a dangerous driver 6. a strict teacher
Can you describe places?	Your best friend just won a free trip for two to anywhere in the world and wants to take you along. Help him or her to decide where to go by describing the following places: 1. San Antonio, Texas 2. San Diego, California 3. Ponce, Puerto Rico 4. Seville, Spain 5. Mexico City, Mexico 6. Cuenca, Ecuador

 For an **online self-test**, go to **go.hrw.com**.

WV3 CALIFORNIA-12

CAPÍTULO 12

Holt Spanish 2 ¡Ven conmigo!, Chapter 12

CAPÍTULO

12 Veranos pasados, veranos por venir

■ TERCER PASO Student Make-Up Assignments Checklist

Pupil's Edition, pp. 359–361

Study the expressions in the **Así se dice** box on page 360: saying when you're going to do something. You should know how to say when you're going to do something.	☐ For additional practice, do Activities 12, 16, pp. 140, 142 in the **Cuaderno de actividades.** ☐ For additional practice, do Activities 15–16, p. 104 in the **Cuaderno de gramática.** ☐ For additional practice, do Activity 6, CD 3 in the **Interactive CD-ROM Tutor.**
Study the expressions in the **Vocabulario** box on page 360: cuando...	☐ For additional practice, do Activities 13–15, pp. 140–141 in the **Cuaderno de actividades.**
Study the grammar presentation in the **Nota gramatical** box on page 360: the subjunctive in the phrase **cuando vuelva a casa...**	☐ Do Activity 27, p. 360, as a writing activity. ☐ Do Activity 28, p. 361. ☐ Do Activity 29, p. 361, as a writing activity. ☐ Do Activity 30, p. 361. ☐ For additional practice, do Activity 7, p. 367 in **Más práctica gramatical.** ☐ For additional practice, do Activities 20–21, p. 106 in the **Cuaderno de gramática.**

CAPÍTULO 12

◼ TERCER PASO Self-Test

Can you say when you're going to do something?	Look at the pictures in Activity 6 of **A ver si puedo...** on page 370 in your textbook. Say when the people in them are going to do the activities pictured. Use these expressions and others you know. antes de cuando termine después de cuando vuelva a para fines de pronto

 For an **online self-test**, go to **go.hrw.com**.

WV3 CALIFORNIA-12

CAPÍTULO 12

Holt Spanish 2 ¡Ven conmigo!, Chapter 12

Quizzes

Nombre _____ Clase _____ Fecha _____

1 Mis amigos y yo

Alternative Quiz 1-1A

Maximum Score: 35

PRIMER PASO

Grammar and Vocabulary

A. Azucena is filling in her address book. Write out the missing parts of the phone numbers of some of her friends. Spell all numbers as words. (8 points)

Fátima	9-48-10-15
Rogelio	7-60-75-22
Antonia	4-51-19-11
Esmeralda	3-34-90-83
Linda	8-12-20-33

1. El número de Antonia es el cuatro, cincuenta y uno,

   _____ , _____ .

2. El número de Esmeralda es el tres,

   _____ , noventa, _____ .

3. El número de Fátima es el nueve, cuarenta y ocho, diez, _____ .

4. El número de Rogelio es el siete, _____ , setenta y cinco,

   _____ .

5. El número de Linda es el ocho, _____ , veinte, treinta y tres.

SCORE [   ]

B. Ricardo's pen pals sent him currency from their home countries. Using the information in the chart, write the nationality of the person or people who sent each bill. Remember to use the correct form of the adjective. (12 points)

MONEDA	PAÍS
colón	Costa Rica
quetzal	Guatemala
lempira	Honduras
nuevo peso	Uruguay
bolívar	Venezuela
euro	España
nuevo sol	Perú
dólar	Puerto Rico

6. Los bolívares son de Alberto y Lucía. Ellos son

   _____ .

7. Los colones son de Óscar. Él es

   _____ .

8. Los quetzales son de Marta. Ella es

   _____ .

9. Los lempiras son de María y Fermín. Ellos son _____ .

10. Los nuevos pesos son de Silvia y Ana. Ellas son _____ .

11. Los dólares son de Daniela y Gerardo. Ellos son _____ .

CAPÍTULO 1

Alternative Quiz 1-1A

12. Los nuevos soles son de Julio. Él es _____ .

13. Los euros son de Hortensia. Ella es _____ .

SCORE [   ]

C. René is asking Anabel and Rosa about their family. Complete their conversation with the correct forms of **tener.** (5 points)

RENÉ   Yo **14.** _____ cinco hermanos. ¿Cuántos hermanos

            15. _____ ustedes?

ANABEL   Somos tres en total. Nosotras **16.** _____ una hermana más, Sonia.

RENÉ   ¿Y cuántos años **17.** _____ ella?

ANABEL   Dieciséis.

RENÉ   Pero Rosa, tú **18.** _____ dieciséis también, ¿no?

ROSA   Sí, Sonia y yo somos gemelas *(twins)*.

SCORE [   ]

D. Everyone in Salvador's family resembles each other in certain ways. Explain their similarities, using the information given and the correct form of the adjectives. (10 points)

19. José Luis es <u>atlético</u> y <u>cómico</u>. Sus primos también son

_____ y _____ .

20. Salvador es <u>pelirrojo</u> y <u>joven</u>. Sus hermanitas también son

_____ y _____ .

21. Doña Antonieta es <u>canosa</u> e <u>inteligente</u>. Su esposo también es

_____ e _____ .

22. Don Fernando es <u>trabajador</u> y <u>simpático</u>. Su hermana también es

_____ y _____ .

23. Toño es <u>alto</u> y <u>leal</u>. Todos sus hijos también son

_____ y _____ .

SCORE [   ]

       Holt Spanish 2 ¡Ven conmigo!, Chapter 1

CAPÍTULO 1

Mis amigos y yo

CAPÍTULO 1

■ SEGUNDO PASO

Maximum Score: 35

Grammar and Vocabulary

A. Everyone has plans for Saturday. Explain at what time people are going out and what they are going to do. Use the correct forms of **salir** and **ir + a +** infinitive and the information in the chart. (10 points)

MODELO   Luis sale a las ocho y media de la mañana. Va a visitar a sus abuelos.

Luis	8:30 a.m.	visitar a sus abuelos
Hortensia	9:00 a.m.	nadar
Julio y Rubén	10:00 a.m.	asistir al partido
yo	12:30 p.m.	ir al centro comercial
tú	4:00 p.m	correr en el parque
mis amigos y yo	7:15 p.m	ver una película

1. Hortensia _____ .

2. Julio y Rubén _____ .

3. Yo _____ .

4. Tú _____ .

5. Mis amigos y yo _____ .

SCORE ☐

B. Complete David's description of the park with the correct form of the verbs in parentheses. (10 points)

El parque es mi lugar favorito. Me gusta **6.** _____ (mirar) a las personas que

7. _____ (correr) con sus perros o que **8.** _____ (descansar)

en las bancas *(benches)*. Los fines de semana mis amigos y yo **9.** _____

(pasar) el rato en el parque. A veces Juana **10.** _____ (tocar) música mexicana

con su guitarra. Cuando yo **11.** _____ (recibir) cartas de mi amiga Carmen, voy al

parque para leerlas. Yo **12.** _____ (buscar) un lugar bonito y **13.**

_____ (abrir) la carta. Carmen **14.** _____ (vivir) en Sevilla.

Ella siempre dice que yo **15.** _____ (deber) visitarla algún día.

SCORE ☐

CAPÍTULO 1

 Alternative Quiz 1-2A

C. Complete what people say on the bus ride home with the correct form of the most logical verb from the box. Use each verb only once. (15 points)

| cuidar | ir | hacer | cortar | sacar |
| comer | regresar | asistir | venir | preparar |

—Vicente, ¿**16.** _____ a mi casa esta tarde?

—Gracias, pero no puedo. Los martes **17.** _____ al restaurante para trabajar.

Después **18.** _____ a mi hermanito en casa.

—Leticia, ¿qué **19.** _____ esta tarde?

—Pues, los martes Sandra y yo siempre **20.** _____ a nuestra clase de baile.

Después nosotras **21.** _____ algo en el café.

—¡Siempre tengo que ayudar en casa! **22.** _____ la basura todos los días y

los sábados **23.** _____ el césped.

—Yo también. Y cuando mi hermano y yo **24.** _____ a casa después de

clases, nosotros **25.** _____ la cena.

SCORE [   ]

TOTAL SCORE [/35]

CAPÍTULO 1

1 Mis amigos y yo

TERCER PASO

Alternative Quiz 1-3A

Maximum Score: 30

Grammar and Vocabulary

A. Complete the statements about what people in Gabriela's family like to eat and drink with the most logical phrase. (6 points)

_____ 1. A mi hermano no le gusta la fruta. De postre, él prefiere comer...
  a. un plátano
  b. una manzana
  c. un flan

_____ 2. A todos nosotros nos encanta la pizza. A mí me gusta la pizza de...
  a. jamón y queso
  b. batido
  c. crema de maní

_____ 3. No me gustan las verduras, pero me encanta...
  a. la lechuga
  b. la fruta
  c. la cebolla

_____ 4. Los domingos, mi papá prepara un desayuno fuerte para toda la familia. Desayunamos...
  a. ensalada de frutas
  b. cereal con leche
  c. huevos con tocino y pan tostado

_____ 5. Mi fruta favorita es...
  a. la toronja
  b. el tocino
  c. la papa

_____ 6. Y mi hermana es vegetariana. Ella come...
  a. muchas salchichas
  b. mucho pollo
  c. muchas legumbres

SCORE [   ]

B. Yadira and Luisa are talking about sports. Complete their conversation with the correct indirect object pronouns: **me, te, le, nos,** or **les.** (12 points)

YADIRA   Mis hermanos siempre hablan del fútbol. A ellos **7.** _____ encanta ver los partidos en la tele todos los domingos. Y a mi padre

8. _____ fascina el béisbol. A mí no **9.** _____

gustan para nada ni el fútbol ni el béisbol. ¡Qué aburridos!

LUISA   Pero Yadira, a ti **10.** _____ gusta el voleibol, ¿verdad? Es mi

deporte favorito. Mi hermana y yo lo jugamos mucho. ¡A nosotras

11. _____ encanta!

Alternative Quiz 1-3A

YADIRA   El voleibol está bien, pero a mí **12.** _____ gustan más otros

deportes, como el ciclismo o el atletismo.

LUISA   A mis amigas y a mí **13.** _____ gusta ir al parque los sábados para

pasear en bici. ¿A tí **14.** _____ gustaría ir con nosotras este sábado?

YADIRA   Sí, por supuesto.

SCORE [   ]

C. What do people think of the cafeteria food? Read people's opinions, then complete the statements below with the correct indirect object pronouns and forms of **gustar, encantar,** or **chocar.** (12 points)

Nombre	Opinión
Sandro	¡Las hamburguesas son fabulosas!
Berta y Marcia	¡La pizza es terrible!
yo	Las enchiladas... ¡qué ricas!
mis amigos y yo	¡Uf! Los sándwiches son horribles.
Lourdes	Siempre compro las galletas de chocolate.
el profesor Hidalgo y la profesora Sánchez	Las ensaladas de frutas son muy malas.

15. A mí _____ _____ las enchiladas.

16. A Sandro _____ _____ las hamburguesas.

17. A Berta y a Marcia _____ _____ la pizza.

18. Al profesor Hidalgo y a la profesora Sánchez _____

_____ las ensaladas de frutas.

19. A mis amigos y a mí, no _____ _____ para nada los

sándwiches.

20. A Lourdes _____ _____ las galletas de chocolate.

SCORE [   ]

TOTAL SCORE [/30]

Holt Spanish 2 ¡Ven conmigo!, Chapter 1

2 Un viaje al extranjero

CAPÍTULO

Alternative Quiz 2-1A

Maximum Score: 35

■ PRIMER PASO

Grammar and Vocabulary

A. This year your Spanish class is taking a two-week study trip to Mexico. Explain how everyone feels before leaving. Complete the sentences with the correct forms of **sentirse** and the adjectives given. (10 points)

1. James y yo _____ _____ (nervioso).

2. Beto y Daniel _____ _____ (preocupado).

3. Sally, tú _____ _____ (emocionado), ¿verdad?

4. También yo _____ _____ (feliz).

5. La profesora _____ _____ (cansado).

SCORE _____

B. Beatriz is planning a goodbye party for José, who is going to study in Mexico. Complete her description of the preparations with the correct form of **estar.** (7 points)

Yo **6.** _____ muy contenta porque mis amigas Luisa y Concha

7. _____ aquí este el fin de semana. Ellas me **8.** _____

ayudando a organizar la fiesta. Ahora Luisa **9.** _____ en la sala, colgando

los globos. Concha y yo **10.** _____ en la cocina, preparando la comida.

Muchos de nuestros amigos vienen a la fiesta para **11.** _____ con José.

Desgraciadamente, mi amigo Ricardo no puede venir porque **12.** _____

enfermo.

SCORE _____

CAPÍTULO 2

Alternative Quiz 2-1A

C. Juan José and Laura are talking after school about their biology class. Put their conversation in order by writing the correct letter, **a–h**, next to each part of the conversation. (8 points)

Juan José

13. _____ —¿Por qué no hablas con la profesora? Ella te puede ayudar, ¿no?

14. _____ —¿Por qué estás preocupada?

15. _____ —Pues, no estoy muy ocupado esta tarde. ¿Qué tal si estudiamos juntos para el examen?

16. _____ —Hola, Laura. Pero... ¿qué te pasa? ¿Estás triste?

Laura

17. _____ —Ya hablé con ella. Pero me siento muy nerviosa porque tenemos un examen esta semana.

18. _____ —Hola, Juan José. Sí, estoy mal. Me siento muy preocupada por la clase de biología.

19. _____ —Pues, mis notas en esa clase no son muy buenas, y mis padres están enfadados conmigo.

20. _____ —Ay, gracias, Juan José. Me gustaría estudiar contigo. ¡Ya me siento más tranquila!

SCORE [　　　　]

D. Read each person's situation, then summarize each using the correct forms of **estar** and one of the expressions from the box. Use each expression only once. (10 points)

de mal humor	de buen humor	tranquilo
emocionado	deprimido	

21. ¡Pobre Enrique! Pronto su mejor amigo va a vivir en otra ciudad.

Él _____ .

22. Cecilia y Carlos sacaron "A" en el examen de geometría.

Ellos _____ .

23. Lucía no puede salir porque tiene que limpiar su cuarto. ¡Qué frustrante!

Ella _____ .

24. Mañana Estela va a celebrar su cumpleaños con una fiesta grande. ¡Va a ser fabulosa!

Ella _____ .

25. Hay un examen mañana, pero Andrea y yo no estamos nerviosos para nada. Al contrario—estudiamos mucho para el examen.

Nosotros _____ .

SCORE [　　　　]　　TOTAL SCORE [　　　　] /35

CAPÍTULO 2

2 Un viaje al extranjero

SEGUNDO PASO

Alternative Quiz 2-2A

Maximum Score: 35

Grammar and Vocabulary

A. Darío had a pool party last weekend. Complete his description of the party with the correct preterite forms of the verbs in parentheses. (9 points)

La fiesta fue excelente. Yo **1.** _____ (preparar) mucha comida rica. Celia

2. _____ (bailar) con Enrique, y Marta y Sandra **3.** _____

(nadar) en la piscina. Todos nosotros **4.** _____ (escuchar) música y después

5. _____ (jugar) al voleibol en la piscina. Y mis padres **6.**

_____ (sacar) unas fotos muy divertidas de todos los invitados.

SCORE [____]

B. Patricia is looking over the calendar for September. Today is Wednesday, September 12. Write the Spanish words and expressions that correspond to the dates given below. (10 points)

domingo	lunes	martes	miércoles	jueves	viernes	sábado
2	3	4	5	6	7	8
9	10	11	12 ★	13	14	15

7. miércoles, el 12 de septiembre: _____

8. martes, el 11 de septiembre: _____

9. domingo, el 2 de septiembre hasta sábado, el 8 _____

10. martes, el 11 de septiembre por la noche _____

11. lunes, el 10 de septiembre: _____

SCORE [____]

Alternative Quiz 2-2A

C. Complete the conversation between Dolores and Delia with the correct present-tense forms of **querer** and **poder**. (6 points)

DOLORES Delia, ¿12. _____ (querer) ir al cine conmigo esta tarde?

DELIA Gracias, pero no 13. _____ (poder). Mi mamá

14. _____ (querer) mi ayuda con la cena esta noche. Por eso, yo

15. _____ (querer) ir al supermercado esta tarde.

DOLORES Entonces, ¿tú 16. _____ (poder) ir al cine mañana?

DELIA Creo que sí. ¿17. _____ (Poder) nosotras ver la nueva película de horror?

DOLORES Sí, está bien.

SCORE [   ]

D. Daniel is leaving for his exchange program next week, and his whole family has been helping him get ready. Write his explanations about where people went, using the correct preterite form of **ir** and the cues given. (5 points)

18. mi hermano y yo/tienda de ropa

_____

19. mis padres/banco

_____

20. mi hermano/agencia de viajes

_____

21. mamá y yo/almacén

_____

22. yo/librería

_____

SCORE [   ]

TOTAL SCORE [   ] /35

Holt Spanish 2 ¡Ven conmigo!, Chapter 2

CAPÍTULO 2

CAPÍTULO 2

Un viaje al extranjero

■ TERCER PASO

Maximum Score: 35

Grammar and Vocabulary

A. Sandra is new in town. Explain to her where the places pictured are in relation to one another, using the expressions in the box. Each expression will be used at least once. (9 points)

lejos	debajo
cerca	
al lado	encima

1. El restaurante está _____ del cine.

2. El cine está _____ del gimnasio.

3. La tienda está _____ del supermercado.

4. La librería está _____ del supermercado.

5. La librería está _____ de la tienda.

6. El gimnasio está _____ del supermercado.

SCORE _____

B. Write the corresponding word next to each definition. (10 points)

el rascacielos	el edificio	el centro
el océano		la montaña

7. El lugar donde puedes nadar, bucear e ir de vela. _____

8. La palabra para lugares como los colegios, las oficinas, la biblioteca, etcétera.

_____

9. La parte de la ciudad donde hay muchas tiendas y oficinas. _____

Alternative Quiz 2-3A

10. El lugar donde puedes esquiar en el invierno. _____

11. Un edificio muy alto. _____

SCORE [   ]

C. Imagine that you are in each of the places pictured below in Activity D. Explain what clothing you need in each place. Mention two items of clothing in each sentence. (8 points)

12. _____

13. _____

14. _____

15. _____

SCORE [   ]

D. Write a sentence describing the weather in each scene. Explain whether it's hot, cold, or cool, and what the other conditions are in each place. (8 points)

Houston

Boulder

Boston

Fairbanks

16. _____

_____

17. _____

_____

18. _____

_____

19. _____

_____

SCORE [   ]

TOTAL SCORE [   ] /35

CAPÍTULO 2

Nombre _____ Clase _____ Fecha _____

La vida cotidiana

■ PRIMER PASO

Maximum Score: 30

Grammar and Vocabulary

A. How are things done at Toña's house? Complete her description by forming adverbs from the adjectives in parentheses. (5 points)

1. A mí, me gusta levantarme y vestirme _____ . (lento)

2. Pero mi hermana se levanta _____ después de despertarse. (inmediato)

3. Mamá _____ prepara el café y papá hace el pan tostado. (general)

4. Papá casi siempre desayuna _____ porque tiene que estar en el trabajo a las nueve. (rápido)

5. Pero _____ , desayunamos todos juntos. (típico)

SCORE ☐

B. What does Marcia need to buy at the drugstore before leaving on her trip to Mexico? Write the Spanish words for the items pictured below. (6 points)

6. _____   7. _____   8. _____

9. _____   10. _____   11. _____

SCORE ☐

Alternative Quiz 3-1A

C. Complete Luis Enrique's description of the morning routine at his house with the Spanish equivalents of the verbs. Choose from the verbs in the box, and use each verb only once. Remember to use the correct reflexive pronoun. (14 points)

afeitarse	cepillarse los dientes	ducharse	despertarse
levantarse	secarse el pelo	mirarse en el espejo	

Durante la semana, mi hermano y yo _____ temprano, a las
                                                    12. *(wake up)*

seis y media. Me levanto inmediatamente. Voy al baño para

_____ . Después _____ y
        13. *(shower)*   **14.** *(I shave)*

_____ . Mi hermano es perezoso y no
        15. *(brush my teeth)*

_____ hasta las siete. Casi siempre mis hermanas necesitan
        16. *(gets up)*

usar el baño a la misma hora, y ellas pasan horas allí.

_____ , se maquillan, _____
        17. *(They dry their hair)*   **18.** *(they look at themselves in the mirror)*

... ¡Qué frustrante!

SCORE _____

D. What time does everyone get dressed at Cecilia's house? Complete what she says with the correct forms of **vestirse.** Remember to use the correct reflexive pronoun. (5 points).

Mamá y Papá **19.** _____ muy temprano, a las siete. Yo

20. _____ a las ocho. Mi hermano **21.** _____

después de desayunar. Los fines de semana, mi hermano y yo no

22. _____ hasta las once o las doce. ¿A qué hora

23. _____ tú los fines de semana?

SCORE _____

TOTAL SCORE _____ /30

CAPÍTULO 3

CAPÍTULO 3

La vida cotidiana

■ SEGUNDO PASO

Maximum Score: 35

Grammar and Vocabulary

A. Answer your pesky little brother's questions about when you're going to do your chores using the cues in parentheses. Remember to use direct object pronouns in your answers. (10 points)

1. ¿Cuándo vas a tender las camas? (ahora mismo)

   _____

2. ¿Cuándo vas a regar las flores? (el domingo)

   _____

3. ¿Cuándo vas a limpiar tu cuarto? (el lunes)

   _____

4. ¿Cuándo vas a lavar los platos? (después de cenar)

   _____

5. ¿Cuándo vas a pasar la aspiradora? (el sábado)

   _____

SCORE _____

B. Before Inés and her friends can go out this afternoon, they all need to do some chores at home. Complete the statements about what everyone has to do with the missing words from the box. Use each word only once. (8 points)

regar	el cuarto de baño	ordenar	el polvo
barrer		tender	el césped	quitar

¡Pobre Inés! Ella necesita 6. _____ su cuarto y

7. _____ su cama. ¿Y Efraín? Pues, él tiene que limpiar

8. _____ . Después, tiene que cortar 9. _____ . Andrés

tiene que sacudir 10. _____ de los muebles en la sala y

11. _____ el piso también. Marisa debe 12. _____ la

mesa y 13. _____ el jardín.

SCORE _____

CAPÍTULO 3

Alternative Quiz 3-2A

C. The Durán children are staying with their grandparents, who are very strict about chores. Look at the chart showing who did what chores today, then answer the grandmother's questions. Use the information in the chart and direct object pronouns in your answers. (10 points)

barrer el piso	Imelda y Rodolfo
limpiar las ventanas	Manuel
preparar el desayuno	Rodolfo
ordenar los cuartos	Imelda, Rodolfo y Manuel
cortar el césped	Imelda

14. ¿Quién limpió las ventanas? _____

15. ¿Quién preparó el desayuno? _____

16. ¿Quiénes ordenaron los cuartos? _____

17. ¿Quién cortó el césped? _____

18. ¿Quiénes barrieron el piso? _____

SCORE _____

D. Arturo and his sister Yasmín are disagreeing about who is supposed to do what chore today. Complete what they say with **me toca, te toca,** or **le toca.** (7 points)

ARTURO   Oye, ¿a quién **19.** _____ barrer el suelo? ¿Tal vez a Azucena?

YASMÍN   No, hoy a Azucena **20.** _____ sacar la basura. A ti

21. _____ barrer el suelo hoy, ¿no?

ARTURO   No, no es así. Yo barro el suelo los martes y los jueves. **22.** _____ a ti, hermanita.

YASMÍN   No, hoy a mí **23.** _____ quitar la mesa.

ARTURO   Pues, no es justo. No voy a barrer el suelo, porque ya tengo muchas cosas que hacer.

Hoy a mí **24.** _____ regar el jardín y también lavar los platos.

YASMÍN   Habla con mamá, entonces, porque yo no voy a barrer el suelo tampoco. A mí también

25. _____ hacer muchos quehaceres.

SCORE _____

TOTAL SCORE _____ /35

Holt Spanish 2 ¡Ven conmigo!, Chapter 3

CAPÍTULO 3

CAPÍTULO 3 La vida cotidiana

■ TERCER PASO

Grammar and Vocabulary

A. Read what different people are interested in, then say what they do in their free time. Use each activity from the list once, and remember to use the correct form of the verb. (12 points)

> hacer monopatín
> usar la computadora
> coleccionar estampillas
> jugar en un equipo de voleibol
> bucear y nadar
> tocar con la banda
> reunirse con amigos
> trabajar en mecánica

1. Andrea quiere ser programadora de computadoras en el futuro.

   _____

2. A Juan Carlos le fascina ir muy rápido.

   _____

3. En sus ratos libres, Yadira siempre va al lago o a la playa.

   _____

4. A mis amigos Darío y Carlota les encanta el voleibol.

   _____

5. A Hortensia le encanta recibir cartas de sus amigos en otros países.

   _____

6. A Marta y a Juan David les interesan los carros.

   _____

7. A Jaime le encanta pasar tiempo con sus amigos.

   _____

8. Leticia y yo estamos locos por la música.

   _____

SCORE [   ]

B. Joel and Azucena have some hobbies and pastimes in common, as well as some different ones. Read the description, then write the name(s) of the person who has each hobby or pastime below. (8 points)

Joel y Azucena tienen muchos pasatiempos. A Joel le gustan todos los deportes, especialmente el monopatín. Durante el verano, se reúne con sus amigos en el parque para hacer monopatín todos los sábados. En el invierno, va al lago mucho para patinar. Azucena prefiere los videojuegos o jugar a las cartas con sus amigos. A Joel le interesan las películas latinoamericanas y europeas. Le gustaría ser director de cine algún día. A los dos amigos les encanta coleccionar estampillas y monedas de muchos países. Azucena toca el piano, y está loca por la música clásica. Toca con la banda de su escuela, y le encanta asistir a conciertos todos los fines de semana.

9. skating _____

10. playing cards _____

11. band _____

12. skateboarding _____

CAPÍTULO 3

Alternative Quiz 3-3A

13. collecting stamps and coins _____

14. videogames _____

15. films and filmmaking _____

16. classical music _____

SCORE [   ]

C. Dolores did a poll of her classmates' hobbies. Look at the poll, then write a sentence explaining how long each person or group has been doing that hobby. (10 points)

Dolores	coleccionar monedas	3 años
Inés	hacer monopatín	7 meses
Fermín y Dolores	tocar con la banda	2 años
Ricardo	bucear	1 año
Ángel	jugar videojuegos	4 años

17. Ángel/jugar videojuegos _____

18. Ricardo/bucear _____

19. Fermín y Dolores/tocar con la banda _____

20. Inés/hacer monopatín _____

21. Dolores/coleccionar monedas _____

SCORE [   ]

D. Your friend Darío is going to interview Carmen, the exchange student, for the school paper. Help Darío out by completing his interview questions with the Spanish equivalents for the English expressions. (5 points)

22. Carmen, ¿ _____ estudias inglés?
    (how long have)

23. ¿Cuáles son tus _____ favoritos?
    (pastimes)

24. ¿ _____ los deportes?
    (Are you interested in)

25. También _____ el monopatín, ¿verdad?
    (you're crazy about)

26. ¿Y cuándo _____ a tocar la guitarra?
    (did you begin)

SCORE [   ]   TOTAL SCORE [   ] /35

Holt Spanish 2 ¡Ven conmigo!, Chapter 3

CAPÍTULO 3

¡Adelante con los estudios!

PRIMER PASO

Alternative Quiz 4-1A

Maximum Score: 35

Grammar and Vocabulary

A. Alberto is starting high school this year, and is nervous about doing well. Answer his questions by telling him what he should and shouldn't do. Use **deberías** and the cues in parentheses. (4 points)

1. ¿Debo preocuparme cuando cometo errores? (no)

   _____

2. ¿Debo hacer muchas preguntas en clase? (sí)

   _____

3. ¿Debo estudiar todas las noches? (sí)

   _____

4. ¿Debo hacer la tarea con mis amigos por correo electrónico? (no)

   _____

SCORE [ ]

B. Adela is interviewing Alicia, a new student, for the school paper. Complete their conversation with the missing expressions from the box. Use each expression once. (7 points)

mi opinión	crees que	para mí	tu opinión
creo que	me parece	qué te parece	

ADELA   Hola, Alicia, y gracias por la entrevista. Alicia, explícame... En

5. _____ , ¿son más o menos fáciles las clases aquí?

ALICIA   Pues, 6. _____ las clases aquí son más difíciles. Y también

7. _____ los profesores son más estrictos. Pero en

8. _____ , eso es bueno.

ADELA   ¿De veras? ¿Y por qué 9. _____ es bueno tener profesores estrictos?

ALICIA   Porque así nosotros aprendemos más.

ADELA   ¿Y el colegio? ¿10. _____ nuestro colegio?

ALICIA   El colegio 11. _____ estupendo, de verdad.
Los estudiantes son inteligentes y amables.

SCORE [ ]

CAPÍTULO 4

 Alternative Quiz 4-1A

C. This year you're an assistant in the school counselor's office. Complete the poster below about good study habits with the missing words. (12 points)

Para 12. _____ buenas notas y ser buen estudiante, hay que...

- 13. _____ toda la materia antes de los exámenes
- aprender 14. _____ la materia
- 15. _____ muchas preguntas
- tomar buenos 16. _____
- 17. _____ la tarea
- 18. _____ las instrucciones de los profesores

¡Y recuerda que es necesario 19. _____ errores para aprender!

SCORE [   ]

D. Two teachers are discussing some students. Complete what they say with the correct present-tense form of the missing verbs. Use each verb only once. (12 points)

---

aprobar   dejar   prestar   olvidar
    suspender   copiar   perder   preocuparse

—Sabes, yo 20. _____ por dos estudiantes. Tengo problemas con ellos

porque no me escuchan y no 21. _____ atención en clase. Casi nunca

22. _____ los exámenes; la semana pasada sacaron muy malas notas. Y

creo que ellos 23. _____ la tarea de sus compañeros. Pienso que van a

24. _____ la clase. Por otro lado, nunca tengo problemas con Ana, la

nueva estudiante. Creo que sigue muy bien las instrucciones y casi nunca

25. _____ sus libros o su tarea.

—¡Qué curioso! En mi clase, Ana es una chica muy desorganizada. Ella

26. _____ la tarea o los libros en casa. Por eso, muchas veces ella llega

tarde y 27. _____ parte de la lección. No sé qué hacer con ella.

SCORE [   ]

TOTAL SCORE [   ] /35

Holt Spanish 2 ¡Ven conmigo!, Chapter 4

CAPÍTULO

4

¡Adelante con los estudios!

CAPÍTULO 4

Alternative Quiz 4-2A

■ SEGUNDO PASO

Maximum Score: 30

Grammar and Vocabulary

A. Angélica and Benjamín are in the cafeteria talking about classmates and teachers. Complete their conversation with the correct forms of **ser** and **estar**. (15 points)

ANGÉLICA Benjamín ¿qué te parece la clase de álgebra? ¿Te gusta la profesora?

BENJAMÍN Pues, sí. Ella **1.** _____ exigente, pero justa. Hoy ella

2. _____ enferma, y por eso tenemos clase con el profesor Peña.

ANGÉLICA Oye, ¿quién **3.** _____ esa chica delgada y morena allí? ¿La chica

que **4.** _____ al lado de Sofía?

BENJAMÍN Se llama Beatriz. Ella y Sofía **5.** _____ primas.

6. _____ de México, pero este año ella **7.** _____
aquí para estudiar y aprender inglés.

ANGÉLICA ¿Y quién es el chico alto que **8.** _____ hablando con ellas?

BENJAMÍN ¿No lo conoces? Es Benito, el hermano de Sofía. **9.** _____ un

chico muy simpático. Por cierto, él y yo **10.** _____ en la misma
clase de álgebra. Benito siempre me ayuda con la tarea.

SCORE [_____]

B. Carlos' family recently moved to a new town. Complete his sentences about who his family members know, and what things they know about, with the correct forms of **conocer**. Remember to include the personal **a** if necessary. (7 points)

11. Papá y mamá _____ bien el centro, pero yo no.

12. Mamá ya _____ las familias que viven al lado.

13. Papá _____ el sistema del metro.

14. Mi hermana Berta y yo _____ un café bueno cerca del colegio.

15. Quiero _____ los estudiantes en todas mis clases.

16. Yo ya _____ todos los estudiantes de mi clase de inglés.

17. Y tú, ¿ya _____ todos tus nuevos compañeros de clase?

SCORE [_____]

CAPÍTULO 4

Alternative Quiz 4-2A

C. Describe each person or group pictured using the correct form of the most logical adjective. Use each adjective only once. (8 points)

| responsable | creativo | generoso | torpe | exigente | entusiasta | aplicado | flojo |

18. Leo y Nuria

_____

19. Los estudiantes

_____

20. El sargento

_____

21. Antonio

_____

22. María Elena

_____

23. Alicia

_____

24. Los muchachos

_____

25. Carlos

_____

SCORE [ ]

TOTAL SCORE [/30]

CAPÍTULO

4

¡Adelante con los estudios!

CAPÍTULO 4

Alternative Quiz 4-3A

■ TERCER PASO

Maximum Score: 35

Grammar and Vocabulary

A. Claudia and some friends are organizing an excursion downtown. She's checking with Lucila to make sure everyone has been called and no one has been left out. Write Lucila's answers to Claudia's questions. Use the correct direct object pronoun and the cues in parentheses in your answers. (8 points)

1. Lucila, ¿quién va a invitar a Francisco y Gregorio? (Berta)

   _____

2. ¿Cuándo vas a llamar a Eduardo? (ahora mismo)

   _____

3. ¿Ya te llamó Guillermo? (sí, anoche)

   _____

4. Y me vas a llamar esta tarde, ¿verdad? (sí, a las cuatro)

   _____

   SCORE _____

B. Claudia and her friends had a great time on their excursion, and now her mom is asking her about it. Write Claudia's answers to her mom's questions. Use the correct direct object pronouns and the cues in parentheses. (8 points)

5. ¿A qué hora tomaste el metro para ir al centro? (a las seis)

   _____

6. ¿Quién recomendó la película? (la hermana de Lucila)

   _____

7. ¿Quiénes compraron los boletos de cine? (Francisco y Guillermo)

   _____

8. ¿Quiénes pagaron la cuenta en el café? (todos nosotros)

   _____

   SCORE _____

Alternative Quiz 4-3A

CAPÍTULO 4

C. Carmen had a busy afternoon yesterday. Complete the description of her day with the correct preterite forms of the verbs in the box. One verb will be used more than once. (12 points)

reunirse	ir	hacer	tomar	
	merendar	platicar		mirar

Primero, Carmen llamó por teléfono a su amiga Anita. Ellas **9.** _____ un

rato sobre las clases y sus familias y por fin **10.** _____ planes para ir al centro

esa tarde. A las dos, Carmen **11.** _____ el metro al centro. Ella

12. _____ con Anita en el Café Imperial. Las dos chicas

13. _____ algo en el café, y después de comer, pasearon por el centro y

14. _____ las vitrinas de sus tiendas favoritas. A las cuatro, Anita

15. _____ a una cita con el dentista. Carmen decidió *(decided)* ver una pelícu-

la. Había mucha gente allí y Carmen **16.** _____ cola por casi veinte minutos.

SCORE [   ]

D. Cristóbal and Diego are making plans. Read their conversations, then indicate if the statements that follow are **a) cierto** or **b) falso.** (7 points)

CRISTÓBAL   Oye, Diego... pienso ir al centro esta tarde. Tengo ganas de comprar unos discos compactos. ¿Quieres ir conmigo?

DIEGO   Sí, me encantaría. Quiero ir de compras también. En las vitrinas del Almacén La Perla hay una chaqueta que me gusta mucho.

CRISTÓBAL   Si quieres, paso por ti a las cuatro o las cuatro y media.

DIEGO   No, mejor nos reunimos en el centro, porque tengo una cita con el médico a las tres y media.

CRISTÓBAL   Bien. Entonces voy a tomar el metro, y nos vemos allí.

DIEGO   De acuerdo, entonces quedamos en vernos en la estación de metro, a las cuatro y media. ¿Quieres ir a merendar algo antes de ir de compras?

CRISTÓBAL   Sí, buena idea. Bueno, hasta esta tarde, entonces.

_____ **17.** After going out with his friend, Diego has a doctor's appointment.

_____ **18.** Diego prefers to get together outside the school building.

_____ **19.** Cristóbal offers to come by and pick Diego up.

_____ **20.** Diego doesn't like window shopping.

_____ **21.** The two friends agree to meet in the café.

_____ **22.** Cristóbal prefers to get something to eat after going shopping.

_____ **23.** Cristóbal is going to take the metro downtown.

SCORE [   ]

TOTAL SCORE [   ] /35

CAPÍTULO 5

¡Ponte en forma!

■ PRIMER PASO

Maximum Score: 30

Grammar and Vocabulary

A. Everyone in Ignacio's family went out and did something fun this weekend. Complete his description of where everyone went using the correct preterite forms of **dar.** (5 points)

El sábado por la mañana, el abuelo y papá **1.** _____ un paseo con nuestro

perro. Mi hermana **2.** _____ un paseo por el centro con sus amigas. Por la

tarde, Jaime y yo **3.** _____ un paseo en bicicleta por el parque. El domingo,

me levanté temprano y **4.** _____ una caminata por el campo con el grupo

de senderismo. ¿Y qué hiciste tú este fin de semana? ¿**5.** _____ una

caminata también?

SCORE _____

B. At the health club where you work, you and your coworkers are required to participate in sports and club activities every day. Explain what all of you did last weekend, using the preterite forms of the verbs in parentheses. (12 points)

6. Yo _____ tres millas. Joel y Jorge _____ dos millas, y

   Dolores _____ cuatro millas. (correr)

7. Joel y Jorge _____ a tres clases de artes marciales. Yo

   _____ a una clase de yoga. Y Dolores _____ a dos

   clases de natación. (asistir)

8. Yo _____ con los clientes una vez. Dolores _____

   con los clientes tres veces. Joel y Jorge _____ con los clientes dos

   veces. (comer)

9. Dolores _____ en dos clases de aeróbicos. Yo _____

   en una clase de tenis. Y Joel y Jorge _____ en tres clases de

   remo. (inscribirse)

SCORE _____

CAPÍTULO 5

Alternative Quiz 5-1A

C. Match each thing, activity, or place on the left with the sport or action most logically associated with it on the right. (8 points)

_____ 10. las montañas   **a.** el atletismo

_____ 11. el lago   **b.** hacer abdominales

_____ 12. el karate   **c.** estirarse

_____ 13. la yoga   **d.** las artes marciales

_____ 14. la pista de correr   **e.** sudar

_____ 15. las botas y las mochilas   **f.** el remo

_____ 16. el estómago   **g.** el senderismo

_____ 17. el calor   **h.** escalar

SCORE [   ]

D. During the hiking club's weekend trip, some people slept in tents and others in cabins. Explain where everyone slept using the correct preterite forms of **dormir.** (5 points)

18. ¡Todos nosotros _____ muy mal!

19. Los guías _____ cerca del lago.

20. ¿Tú _____ en una tienda de campaña?

21. Daniela _____ en la cabaña pequeña.

22. Yo _____ en la cabaña grande.

SCORE [   ]

TOTAL SCORE [   ] /30

Holt Spanish 2 ¡Ven conmigo!, Chapter 5

CAPÍTULO 5

Nombre _____ Clase _____ Fecha _____

¡Ponte en forma!

■ SEGUNDO PASO

Maximum Score: 35

Grammar and Vocabulary

A. Someone with a lot of health problems wrote a letter to the advice column of your local paper. Read the letter, then complete the response with the correct negative informal commands. Use the verbs in parentheses. (15 points)

> *Querida Dra. Bienestar,*
>
> *No sé qué hacer. ¡Soy un desastre! Me gustaría ponerme en forma, pero es difícil.*
>
> *Quiero perder peso, pero sigo comiendo mucho. Sé que necesito seguir una dieta y*
>
> *hacer ejercicio, pero cuando comienzo a hacerlo, lo dejo casi en seguida. Prefiero*
>
> *quedarme en casa, para ver la televisión y comer papitas. Y otro problema—no*
>
> *puedo dejar de fumar. ¡Ayúdame!*
>
> *Juan Sinvoluntad*

Querido Juan,

Primero, no **1.** _____ (decir)

que eres un desastre, y no

2. _____ (ser) pesimista.

Aquí tengo unos consejos para ti:

• No **3.** _____ (jugar) con la

salud, pues es la cosa más importante.

• Después de clases, no

4. _____ (estar) en casa

viendo la tele. ¡Ve al parque a caminar!

• No le **5.** _____ (añadir) sal

a la comida.

• No **6.** _____ (fumar) más.

Fumar es muy malo para la salud.

• No **7.** _____ (comer)

muchos dulces ni **8.** _____

(comprar) comida muy grasosa. Si tus

amigos quieren ir a comer pizza o helado,

no **9.** _____ (ir) con ellos.

¡No **10.** _____ (buscar) más

excusas! Ya sabes lo que necesitas hacer.

¡Sigue mis consejos y pronto te vas a sentir

mejor!

SCORE _____

Alternative Quiz 5-2A

B. José is studying for a health test. Help him by matching each term to its corresponding definition. (5 points)

relajarse	el estrés	entrenarse
	hacer régimen	las grasas

11. Lo que las personas sienten cuando tienen mucho trabajo y no duermen lo suficiente:

    _____

12. El acto de practicar mucho para un partido o competencia deportiva:

    _____

13. Lo opuesto de sentirse nervioso: _____

14. Seguir una dieta y comer cosas sanas y bajas en calorías: _____

15. Grupo de comida muy alta en calorías: _____

SCORE [   ]

C. The new trainer at the sports club has a strict plan for you. Write what she tells you to do, using informal commands. (15 points)

CLUB DEPORTIVO OLÍMPICO

Plan de entrenamiento

- 16. _____ (Salir) a caminar todas las tardes.
- 17. _____ (Decir) "adiós" a los dulces.
- 18. _____ (Tener) cuidado al levantar pesas.
- 19. _____ (Saltar) la cuerda 100 veces todos los días.
- 20. _____ (Ir) al gimnasio todos los días.
- 21. _____ (Comer) bien.
- 22. _____ (Evitar) la grasa.
- 23. _____ (Correr) dos millas, tres veces a la semana.
- 24. _____ (Respirar) profundamente después de correr.
- 25. _____ (Hacer) 50 abdominales todas las mañanas.

SCORE [   ]

TOTAL SCORE [   ] /35

CAPÍTULO 5

¡Ponte en forma!

CAPÍTULO 5

Alternative Quiz 5-3A

Maximum Score: 35

■ TERCER PASO

Grammar and Vocabulary

A. A lot of people at school have gotten the flu recently. Explain what people couldn't do this weekend because they had to rest in bed instead. Use the correct form of **poder** in the preterite. (9 points)

1. Yo no _____ jugar al tenis.

2. ¿Y tú? No _____ correr en el parque, ¿verdad?

3. Graciela no _____ asistir a su clase de natación.

4. Nosotros no _____ entrenarnos para el partido.

5. Julio y Gabriela no _____ levantar pesas en el gimnasio.

6. Elena no _____ hacer yoga.

SCORE [____]

B. Write the Spanish word for the parts of the body numbered below. Remember to include the definite article. (12 points)

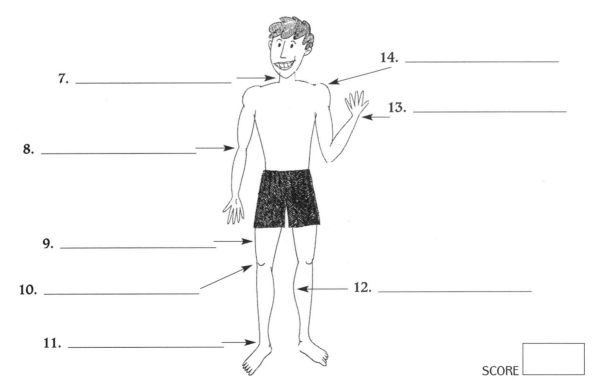

7. _____

8. _____

9. _____

10. _____

11. _____

14. _____

13. _____

12. _____

SCORE [____]

Alternative Quiz 5-3A

C. Complete the sentences about the injuries or aches of the people pictured below. Use the correct form of one of the verbs in the box with the corresponding body part. Use each verb and part of the body only once. (8 points)

> lastimarse   hacerse daño   el hombro   la muñeca
>   la rodilla   tener calambre en   los tobillos   torcerse

Magdalena

15. Magdalena fue al gimnasio y

_____ .

Mario

17. Mario jugó al fútbol esta mañana y

_____ .

Luis y Luisa

16. Luis y Luisa fueron a la pista de correr

y _____ .

Manuel

18. Manuel fue al lago para practicar el remo esta mañana. Ahora

_____ .

SCORE [ ]

D. Inés and some friends had some problems during their recent bike trip. Complete her description of the trip with the correct preterite forms of the verbs in parentheses. (6 points)

Este fin de semana un grupo de amigos y yo fuimos a pasear en bicicleta. ¡Qué desastre!

Primero, Julián no pudo venir porque **19.** _____ (enfermarse) la noche anterior. Luego, al subir una colina *(hill)*, Isabel y yo **20.** _____ (cansarse) y no pudimos seguir. Lorenzo **21.** _____ (olvidarse) de llevar una chaqueta. Por eso, **22.** _____ (quejarse) mucho del frío y lo pasó muy mal. Luego, a las doce, decidimos comer—¡pero yo no comí nada, porque no **23.** _____ (acordarse) de poner mi almuerzo en la mochila! Parece que la única persona que lo pasó bien fue Juanita. Ella

24. _____ (divertirse) mucho porque le encanta pasear en bicicleta.

SCORE [ ]   TOTAL SCORE [/35]

CAPÍTULO 6
De visita en la ciudad

■ PRIMER PASO

Grammar and Vocabulary

A. María and her classmates are getting ready for a field trip, but they still have some questions about details. Complete María's explanation of what everyone needs to find out with the correct forms of **saber**. (5 points)

1. Yo no _____ si quiero visitar el museo o el zoológico primero.

2. Rafael y yo no _____ cúanto dinero necesitamos llevar.

3. La profesora no _____ dónde vamos a almorzar.

4. Marisa y Pedro no _____ a qué hora sale el autobús.

5. ¿Y tú? ¿_____ si todos los estudiantes van o no?

SCORE [____]

B. Marta has a summer job as a bilingual tour guide. Complete what she says about her work with the correct form of **saber** or **conocer**. Include the personal **a** if it's required. (12 points)

¡Me encanta trabajar de guía! El mejor guía del grupo es Néstor, porque él

6. _____ más información que nadie. Cuando nosotros no

7. _____ algo, siempre le hacemos preguntas. Hace ocho años que él trabaja

aquí, y por eso **8.** _____ muchas personas importantes de la ciudad. Por ejem-

plo, él **9.** _____ muchos músicos, y por eso siempre

10. _____ dónde y cuándo hay los mejores conciertos. Yo ya

11. _____ mucho sobre la historia de nuestra ciudad. Todos los días leo libros

y hablo con los otros guías, porque quiero **12.** _____ mucho más. Ya

13. _____ bien el centro, especialmente la parte antigua.

SCORE [____]

CAPÍTULO 6

Alternative Quiz 6-1A

C. Miguel and his family are going to a wedding in the city next weekend. Complete what his sister tells him about their trip with the correct missing words. (12 points)

| guía | lancha | autobuses | turistas |
| conductores | edificios | iglesia | boda |

Miguel, ya sabes que el próximo fin de semana, vamos a la **14.** _____ de tu

prima Margarita. La ceremonia va a ser el sábado, en una **15.** _____ muy

bonita. Después, el domingo vamos al río para hacer una excursión en

16. _____ . Después, vamos con un grupo de **17.** _____ a vi-

sitar los monumentos de la ciudad. El **18.** _____ nos va a explicar todo, y creo

que va a ser muy interesante. ¡Te va a encantar la ciudad! Hay muchos

19. _____ altos y modernos, y las calles están llenas *(full)* de carros, taxis,

motocicletas y **20.** _____ . Todos los **21.** _____ van muy rápido.

SCORE [   ]

D. Pablo works at the Tourist Office. Complete the conversation between him and a tourist with the correct missing Spanish expressions. (6 points)

| por supuesto | disculpe | Me podría decir |
| no estoy seguro | no tengo ni idea | sabe |

TURISTA Señor, **22.** _____ .
excuse me

¿**23.** _____ dónde está el Museo de Antropología?
(Could you tell me)

PABLO Sí, **24.** _____ . Está en la Plaza Colón, al lado del Banco de la
República. *(of course)*

TURISTA ¿Y **25.** _____ usted cuánto cuestan las entradas?
(do you know)

PABLO Pues, **26.** _____ . Creo que cuestan 800 pesos.
(I'm not sure)

TURISTA ¿Y hay descuento para estudiantes?

PABLO Lo siento, pero **27.** _____ .
(I have no idea)

SCORE [   ]   TOTAL SCORE [/35]

CAPÍTULO 6

6 De visita en la ciudad

CAPÍTULO

■ SEGUNDO PASO

Grammar and Vocabulary

A. Complete the description of Nora's upcoming train trip with the missing words. Use each word only once. (12 points)

maletero	andén	taquilla	estación	
pasajeros	boletos	vía	ida y vuelta	

Hoy Nora y Paloma empiezan su viaje por tren de Los Ángeles a San Antonio. La semana pasada, Nora llamó para averiguar el precio de los **1.** _____ . El día antes del viaje, ella

fue a la **2.** _____ de tren con su amiga Paloma. Las dos hicieron cola en la

3. _____ y por fin compraron los boletos. Nora compró uno de

4. _____ , porque piensa regresar a Nueva York en dos semanas. Esta mañana, las

chicas tomaron un taxi a la estación. Un **5.** _____ las ayudó con sus maletas. Las

chicas fueron al **6.** _____ para esperar el tren. Ahora mismo, el tren llega en la

7. _____ número 19. Hay muchos otros **8.** _____ subiéndose al

tren. Nora y Paloma están muy contentas, porque va a ser un viaje fabuloso.

SCORE [   ]

B. Roberto's family had a busy time during their tour of San Antonio. Complete his description of what people did with the correct preterite forms of the verbs in parentheses. (8 points)

Primero, Pilar y yo **9.** _____ (hacer) un recorrido por la Villita. Después,

nosotros **10.** _____ (visitar) el Álamo y más tarde, **11.** _____

(subirse) a una lancha. Mis tíos y mi primito Santiago **12.** _____ (explorar)

primero el Paseo del Río, y luego fueron al zoológico. ¡A Santiago le **13.** _____

(encantar) el zoo! Mi prima Rosa **14.** _____ (decidir) ir primero al Instituto de

Culturas Texanas. Luego, **15.** _____ (sacar) muchas fotos desde la Torre de las

Américas. Más tarde, ella **16.** _____ (ver) las flores y plantas del Jardín Botánico.

SCORE [   ]

CAPÍTULO 6

Alternative Quiz 6-2A

C. Mercedes is in the city on business. Look at her schedule, then complete the sentences about her day. Write the correct missing expression in the first blank and the correct preterite form of the verb in parentheses in the second blank. (10 points)

```
7:00    wake-up call; e-mail office
7:45    breakfast w/ Natalia
9:30    meeting—Jefferson Building
12:00   lunch w/ clients
3:30    catch train home
```

Después	Para empezar	A continuación
Por último	Luego	

17. _____ , Mercedes se despertó a las siete y

_____ (escribir) unas cartas electrónicas.

18. _____ , a las ocho menos cuarto, ella

_____ (reunirse) con su amiga Natalia para desayunar.

19. _____ , ella _____ (ir) al Edificio Jefferson

para ver a unos clientes.

20. _____ , a las doce, ella _____ (comer) con

unos clientes.

21. _____ , ella _____ (subirse) al tren a las

tres y media.

SCORE [   ]

TOTAL SCORE [/30]

CAPÍTULO 6

6 De visita en la ciudad

C A P Í T U L O

Alternative Quiz 6-3A

Maximum Score: 35

■ TERCER PASO

Grammar and Vocabulary

A. Imagine you're dining in a restaurant you've never been to before. What would you say in the following situations? Write a question or statement in Spanish. (10 points)

1. You would like to order a mineral water.

   _____

2. You wonder if the soup is spicy.

   _____

3. You want to know what the waiter recommends.

   _____

4. You want the waiter to bring you flan for dessert.

   _____

5. You would like the waiter to bring you the bill.

   _____

SCORE [   ]

B. Answer the questions about the diners and waiters at Mesón Rivas, based on the drawing. (6 points)

6. ¿A quiénes les sirve el postre Sergio?

   _____

7. ¿Quién le está dejando una propina a

   Alberto? _____

8. En este momento, ¿quiénes están pidiendo

   la cena? _____

9. En total, ¿cuántas personas cenan esta noche

   en el restaurante? _____

Alternative Quiz 6-3A

10. ¿Quiénes son los meseros? _____

11. ¿Quién les trae la cena a Benito y su mamá? _____

SCORE [   ]

C. Andrés writes restaurant reviews for a local paper, and he just visited an awful restaurant. Complete his review with the correct preterite forms of **pedir** and **servir**. (12 points)

¡Qué restaurante tan horrible! Para cenar, mi esposa **12.** _____ (pedir)

una ensalada de frutas... y los meseros le **13.** _____ (servir) una ensalada

de lechuga y tomate. Yo **14.** _____ (pedir) el bistec, pero el mesero me

15. _____ (servir) una hamburguesa. Antonio y Benjamín cenaron con

nosotros. De postre, ellos **16.** _____ (pedir) flan de piña, pero la mesera les

17. _____ (servir) helado de limón. Por último, nosotros

18. _____ (pedir) café, pero ellos nos **19.** _____ (servir) té.

SCORE [   ]

D. Rosaura and some classmates are setting up the food at their school's International Dinner. Complete their conversation about who brought what foods with the correct preterite forms of **traer.** (7 points)

ROSAURA   ¡Cuánta comida! ¿Quién **20.** _____ el flan? ¿Lo

21. _____ tú, Estela?

ESTELA   No, no lo **22.** _____ . Yo **23.** _____ las

tortillas.

ROSAURA   ¿Y las empanadas? ¿Sabes quién las **24.** _____ ?

ALEJANDRO   Las **25.** _____ Sara y yo. Y me parece que Susana

26. _____ el arroz con pollo.

SCORE [   ]

TOTAL SCORE [   ] /35

CAPÍTULO 7

¿Conoces bien tu pasado?

■ PRIMER PASO

Grammar and Vocabulary

A. Teresa is talking about where everyone used to go on summer vacation when they were little. Complete what she says with the correct imperfect form of **ir.** (5 points)

1. Diego y sus hermanos _____ a la playa, a la casa de sus primos.

2. A veces, en agosto yo _____ a la casa de mi amiga Irene en Ponce.

3. Mi amigo Cristóbal _____ a las montañas para visitar a sus tíos.

4. Mi hermana Verónica y yo _____ a San Juan para ver a nuestros abuelos.

5. ¿Y tú? Típicamente _____ a Santo Domingo en julio, ¿verdad?

SCORE _____

B. Benito is inteviewing his great-uncle Carlos about growing up in Ponce. Complete what his great-uncle says with the correct imperfect forms of the verbs in parentheses. (11 points)

En aquel entonces, nosotros **6.** _____ (vivir) en Ponce, donde papá y

mamá **7.** _____ (tener) un pequeño restaurante. Después de clases mi her-

mana y yo **8.** _____ (ayudar) en el restaurante. Siempre me

9. _____ (gustar) estar allí. Nuestros vecinos *(neighbors)* y amigos

10. _____ (venir) casi todos los días a pasar el rato y comer algo. Papá y

mamá **11.** _____ (trabajar) día y noche. ¡Mamá **12.** _____

(saber) preparar los mejores platos de toda la ciudad! Ella y yo **13.** _____

(cocinar) juntos a veces, y a veces yo **14.** _____ (lavar) los platos. Mi her-

mana **15.** _____ (preferir) hablar con la gente, y por eso generalmente ella y

papá **16.** _____ (servir) la comida.

SCORE _____

C. When he was little, Eduardo watched a lot of television with his family. Complete his statements about the programs everyone usually watched, using the correct imperfect form of **ver.** (5 points)

17. Yadira y yo _____ los dibujos animados *(cartoons)* los sábados por la mañana.

18. Y yo _____ muchos programas sobre animales también.

19. Mamá típicamente _____ películas de amor.

20. Papa y tío Pancho siempre _____ partidos de fútbol los domingos.

21. ¿Y tú? Cuando eras joven, ¿ _____ televisión con tu familia?

SCORE [＿＿＿]

D. Explain what everyone generally did in the park when they were little, based on the drawing. Use the correct imperfect form of one of the verbs listed. Each verb will be used once. (14 points)

hacer travesuras   soñar con   construir   trepar a los árboles
asustarse   contar chistes   compartir   pelear

MODELO Yolanda trepaba a los árboles.

22. Mis amigos y yo _____ .

23. Joel _____ .

24. Gregorio _____ .

25. Ignacio y Jaime _____ .

26. José y Juan _____ .

27. Guillermo _____ .

28. Adela _____ .

SCORE [＿＿＿] TOTAL SCORE [＿＿ /35]

CAPÍTULO 7

¿Conoces bien tu pasado?

■ SEGUNDO PASO

Grammar and Vocabulary

A. Complete Antonio's description of his next-door neighbors by choosing the correct word from the choices in parentheses. (8 points)

Julián tiene un perro que se llama Oso. Es bastante viejo; tiene siete

1. _____ (o/u) ocho años. No me gusta Oso porque es un perro travieso

2. _____ (y/e) también impaciente. Cuando Julián sale a caminar con Oso, el

perro quiere correr al parque **3.** _____ (y/e) explorar allí. Cuando Oso era

joven, siempre se le escapaba *(escaped from)* a Julián **4.** _____ (y/e) iba por

todo el pueblo, haciendo travesuras. Julián tiene veintidós **5.** _____ (o/u)

veintitrés años. Estudia lenguas en la universidad. ¡Sabe hablar alemán, japonés

6. _____ (y/e) inglés! En el futuro, a Julián le gustaría trabajar en los Estados

Unidos **7.** _____ (o/u) Europa. Su madre, doña Alicia, es una señora muy

simpática. Es alegre **8.** _____ (y/e) inteligente.

SCORE [   ]

B. Lorenzo is looking at his photo album and describing the way people were when they were younger. Write what he says, using the correct imperfect form of **ser** and the correct form of a logical adjective from the list. Use each adjective once. (14 points)

| bondadoso | egoísta | solitario | conversador |
| consentido | aventurero | impaciente | |

Manuel

Mi primo Luis

Mis amigos y yo

9. _____

_____

10. _____

_____

11. _____

_____

Alternative Quiz 7-2A

CAPÍTULO 7

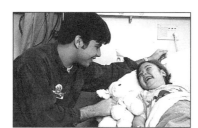

Mi hermano Mario

Mi prima Ana

12. _____

_____

_____

13. _____

_____

_____

Mis hermanas menores

Yo

14. _____

_____

_____

15. _____

_____

_____

SCORE [   ]

C. Miguel's grandmother is describing what the neighborhood used to look like when she was young. Complete what she says with **hay** or **había**. (8 points)

Pues, cuando yo era niña, **16.** _____ una tienda pequeña cerca de nuestra

casa adonde íbamos todos los domingos a comprar dulces. Allí **17.** _____ una

señora muy simpática que siempre nos regalaba dulces. Ahora no **18.** _____

ninguna tienda allí ni nada—sólo **19.** _____ un estacionamiento enorme. ¡Qué

triste! En aquel entonces, la ciudad era pequeña y no **20.** _____ muchos edifi-

cios grandes. Ahora creo que **21.** _____ demasiado tráfico y demasiadas per-

sonas... Claro, hoy en día **22.** _____ más carros en la ciudad que los que

23. _____ en el pasado.

SCORE [   ]

TOTAL SCORE [   ] /30

Holt Spanish 2 ¡Ven conmigo!, Chapter 7

7 ¿Conoces bien tu pasado?

TERCER PASO

Maximum Score: 35

Grammar and Vocabulary

A. You are at a family reunion, listening to everyone describe relatives and neighbors from their child-hoods. Read each description, then choose the comparison that best fits each person. (9 points)

_____ 1. Cuando teníamos problemas, siempre hablábamos con doña Ángela. Era una mujer tan inteligente y respon-sable. Y muy honesta también—siempre nos decía la verdad en todo.

_____ 2. En aquel entonces papá trabajaba en un hospital. Se le vantaba temprano y trabajaba todo el día, el pobre. Le gustaba el trabajo, pero siempre estaba cansado.

_____ 3. Tío Pablo era muy buena persona pero ¡uf!, cómo le gustaba hablar. Y hablaba de cosas que a nadie le interesaban.

_____ 4. Recuerdo que el hijo de doña Angélica era un atleta excelente. Practicaba muchos deportes—el atletismo, la natación, el remo. Era alto y grande, y tenía brazos enormes.

_____ 5. A mi hermana Anabel le encantaba ir a la escuela. Todas las mañanas, ella salía de casa corriendo y cantando.

_____ 6. ¿Y Pedro? Pues, nunca daba problemas, siempre ayudaba en casa, sacaba notas buenas... en fin, era el hijo perfecto.

a. Era tan aburrido como un pato.

b. Era tan noble como un perro.

c. Dormía tan bien como un lirón.

d. Era tan bueno como un ángel.

e. Era tan fuerte como un toro.

f. Era tan feliz como una lombriz.

SCORE _____

B. Rafael made a chart comparing his new school in Texas with his old school in New York. Write a sentence about each item in his chart, making a comparison of equality between the two schools. (12 points)

MODELO Mi colegio aquí es tan moderno como el de Nueva York.

	Texas	Nueva York
el colegio	Es moderno.	También era moderno.
7. los profesores	¡Muy exigentes!	También.
8. los exámenes	¡Qué difíciles son!	Sí, eran muy difíciles.
9. los estudiantes	Me parecen aplicados.	También eran aplicados.
10. la cafetería	¡Es horrible!	También era horrible.
11. las clases	Todas son interesantes.	Sí, también.
12. el director	Creo que es justo.	También me parecía justo.

Alternative Quiz 7-3A

7. _____

8. _____

9. _____

10. _____

11. _____

12. _____

SCORE [   ]

C. Ricardo and Azucena were very competitive when they were growing up, and tried to follow in one another's footsteps exactly. Write comparisons explaining how their competitive spirit led them to do identical things. Follow the model and use the cues given. (14 points)

MODELO quehaceres (hacer)
Azucena hacía tantos quehaceres como Ricardo.

13. notas altas (sacar)

_____

14. instrumentos musicales (tocar)

_____

15. fiestas (ir a)

_____

16. deportes (practicar)

_____

17. tarea (tener)

_____

18. libros (leer)

_____

19. horas al día (estudiar)

_____

SCORE [   ]

TOTAL SCORE [/35]

CAPÍTULO 7

Diversiones

■ PRIMER PASO

Maximum Score: 35

Grammar and Vocabulary

A. Match each word to its corresponding definition. (11 points)

_____1. Es otro nombre para una actriz famosísima.

_____2. Esta atracción es para las personas a quienes les gusta hacer travesuras.

_____3. Es un animal grande, de rayas anaranjadas y negras.

_____4. Es un animal largo y delgado. No tiene patas *(legs)*, pero se puede mover muy rápido.

_____5. Es un animal de muchos colores que a veces sabe hablar.

_____6. Es un animal grande y verde con una boca enorme y muchos dientes.

_____7. Es una atracción ideal para las personas a quienes les gusta subir y bajar muy rápido.

_____8. Es una parte importante de las películas de ciencia-ficción y de aventuras.

_____9. Es un animal que camina muy lento y que típicamente vive muchos años.

_____10. Es un animal inteligente que sabe trepar a los árboles muy bien.

_____11. Si te gusta ver toda la ciudad desde muy alto, esta atracción es perfecta para ti.

a. el tigre

b. la rueda de Chicago

c. el cocodrilo

d. la estrella

e. la montaña rusa

f. el loro

g. la serpiente

h. la tortuga

i. los carros chocones

j. los efectos especiales

k. el mono

SCORE [____]

B. Last week was really intense for Roberto. Complete his description of what happened with the correct **-ísimo/a/os/as** form of the adjectives in parentheses. (12 points)

Estuve 12. _____ (ocupado) la semana pasada. El lunes, mis amigos y yo

fuimos a la nueva pizzería y pedimos unas pizzas 13. _____ (rico). El martes,

tomé un examen en la clase de matemáticas. Fue un examen difícil y 14. _____

(largo). El jueves, fui al centro comercial pero no compré nada porque todo estaba

15. _____ (caro). El viernes, nos dieron los exámenes de matemáticas. Por

suerte, saqué una nota 16. _____ (buena), pero mi amiga Beatriz sacó una C y estuvo **17.** _____ (triste). Vi una película **18.** _____ (aburrido) el

sábado, y por la noche, fui a una fiesta de cumpleaños **19.** _____ (divertido)
para mi amiga Berta.

SCORE [____]

C. Carlota is explaining her opinions about the zoo, amusement park, and some recent films. Express each of her opinions using the correct form of the superlative. (7 points)

MODELO la atracción/cara/todas/la montaña rusa
La atracción más cara de todas es la montaña rusa.

20. monos/traviesos/todos/los pequeños _____

21. loro/inteligente/zoológico/de Guatemala _____

22. animal/feo/todos/el cocodrilo _____

23. actor/guapo/mundo/el nuevo actor cubano _____

24. cola/larga/parque de atracciones/para los carros chocones _____

25. efectos especiales/creativos/festival/los de *Galaxias 2050* _____

26. atracción/aburrida/parque de atracciones/la rueda de Chicago _____

SCORE [____]

D. Santiago and Carmen are talking about a movie they just saw. Complete their comments with the Spanish equivalents of the English superlatives. Remember to use the correct form of the adjective. (5 points)

SANTIAGO La música de la película estuvo buena. Para mí, ese grupo es

27. _____ del país.
(the best)

CARMEN Para mí también. Las dos canciones al final fueron **28.** _____ .
(the best)

SANTIAGO ¡Esa actriz es horrible! Es **29.** _____ del mundo.
(the worst)

CARMEN Sí, y los efectos especiales fueron malísimos también. Creo que fueron

30. _____ de todas las películas de este año.
(the worst)

SANTIAGO En fin, no me gustó la película pero sí me encanta el cine nuevo. Es

31. _____ y el más grande de todos, ¿verdad?
(the best)

SCORE [____] TOTAL SCORE [__/35]

CAPÍTULO 8

CAPÍTULO 8

8 Diversiones

Alternative Quiz 8-2A

■ SEGUNDO PASO

Maximum Score: 35

Grammar and Vocabulary

A. Sebastián's family was preparing to leave for a trip yesterday. Complete his explanations of what everyone was doing to get ready. Use the correct imperfect form of the verbs in parentheses. (8 points)

1. Dolores, ¿por qué _____ (ver) televisión mientras todos nosotros

   _____ (estar) trabajando?

2. Mientras mamá y papá _____ (ir) al banco, yo _____

   (comprar) película y bloqueador en la farmacia.

3. Mientras yo _____ (regar) las flores, mamá le _____ (dar)

   a doña Daniela las instrucciones para cuidar al gato.

4. Mientras papá _____ (llevar) el carro al taller, Sergio y yo

   _____ (hacer) las maletas.

SCORE _____

B. La señora Acosta had a busy day yesterday. Read what she did, then letter the errands below from **a** to **f,** according to the order in which she did them. (9 points)

   Primero la señora Rivas mandó una carta a su hermana y un regalo de cumpleaños a su tía. Después sacó dinero y luego compró aspirinas y un cepillo de dientes. Más tarde, habló con el mecánico sobre los problemas con el carro. Luego fue a la gasolinera. Y por fin estuvo media hora en la sala de espera del dentista, esperando a su hija.

_____ 5. ponerle gasolina al carro

_____ 6. llevar el carro al taller

_____ 7. pasar por el banco

_____ 8. pasar por la farmacia

_____ 9. acompañar a su hija a la cita

_____ 10. pasar por el correo

SCORE _____

CAPÍTULO 8

Alternative Quiz 8-2A

C. Claudia is getting ready for a trip to Puerto Rico. Complete what her friend Cristina says about the trip with the correct preposition from the box. If no preposition is needed, write an **X** in the blank. (18 points)

> en   que   con
> de   a   por

Mi amiga Claudia va **11.** _____ salir para Puerto Rico mañana. Está muy

emocionada porque desde niña, ella siempre soñaba **12.** _____ conocer la isla.

Hablé con Claudia anteayer. Estaba nerviosa porque todavía tenía **13.** _____

hacer muchas cosas. Quería **14.** _____ comprar una maleta nueva y también

necesitaba **15.** _____ ir al banco. Yo le dije: "Claudia, deja

16. _____ preocuparte. Ahora mismo voy a tu casa y te ayudo

17. _____ organizar todo". Entonces, nosotros quedamos

18. _____ vernos a las dos. Ahora sí que está lista para el viaje. Ella comenzó

19. _____ planear el viaje hace dos meses. Pasó **20.** _____ la

agencia de viajes para pedir información y comprar el boleto. Hizo las reservaciones del hotel y

se acordó **21.** _____ comprar regalos para sus parientes en Puerto Rico.

Durante su viaje, espera **22.** _____ ver a sus parientes, ir a la playa y visitar

el Yunque.

SCORE [   ]

TOTAL SCORE [/35]

Holt Spanish 2 ¡Ven conmigo!, Chapter 8

8 CAPÍTULO

Diversiones

■ TERCER PASO

Grammar and Vocabulary

A. Everyone is talking about festivals. Complete the statements with the correct preterite forms of **decir** and the imperfect of the other verbs in parentheses. (10 points)

1. ¿Por qué le _____ (decir/tú) a Benjamín que te _____ (parecer) fea mi máscara? Creo que es muy bonita.

2. Yo le _____ (decir) a mi hermana que no me _____ (gustar) su disfraz para el baile.

3. Nosotros le _____ (decir) a Antonio que nos _____ (encantar) las decoraciones con flores de papel.

4. Alicia y Andrés nos _____ (decir) que les _____ (gustar) las carrozas con músicos.

5. Alejandro me _____ (decir) que le _____ (parecer) muy aburridos los desfiles.

SCORE [   ]

B. Match each word to its corresponding definition. (12 points)

_____ 6. vestido o traje especial que se pone durante un festival

_____ 7. procesión larga por las calles como parte de una celebración

_____ 8. algo que se lleva en la cabeza o delante de la cara

_____ 9. caminar como parte de una procesión o festival

_____ 10. crear, dibujar o pintar algo

_____ 11. divertirse

_____ 12. carros decorados

_____ 13. poner flores y colgar globos

a. desfile

b. carrozas

c. disfraz

d. disfrutar

e. máscara

f. decorar

g. desfilar

h. diseñar

SCORE [   ]

CAPÍTULO 8

Alternative Quiz 8-3A

C. Your class is on a trip to Puerto Rico. Complete what everyone said about the group's plans with the correct preterite forms of **decir.** (8 points)

14. Yo _____ que todos querían asistir a un partido de béisbol.

15. La profesora _____ que íbamos a visitar el Museo Casals mañana.

16. Nuestro guía _____ que el Festival de San Sebastián era fabuloso.

17. Graciela, ¿qué _____ ustedes sobre la posibilidad de visitar Ponce?

18. Tomás, ¿qué _____ tú sobre la excursión a El Yunque?

19. El profesor _____ que teníamos que levantarnos temprano mañana.

20. Alberto y Elena _____ que tenían ganas de ver el Morro primero.

21. Todos nosotros _____ que queríamos comer arroz con habichuelas.

SCORE [   ]

TOTAL SCORE [/30]

CAPÍTULO 8

CAPÍTULO 9

¡Día de mercado!

■ PRIMER PASO

Maximum Score: 30

Grammar and Vocabulary

A. Ángela works at the Tourist Office. Write what she advises visitors to do, forming singular and plural formal commands from the verbs in parentheses. (15 points)

Al señor Riojas: 1. _____ (Levantarse) temprano mañana y

2. _____ (hacer) una excursión al río para pescar.

A la señorita Ibarra: No 3. _____ (olvidarse) de pasar por el Museo del Pueblo.

A los señores Maciel: 4. _____ (Empezar) con una visita a la catedral.

Después, 5. _____ (cruzar) la Playa Mayor y

6. _____ (ir) a la Casa de Cultura.

A la señora Montes: 7. _____ (Dar) un paseo por el Parque Central.

A los señores Garza: 8. _____ (Bajar) tres cuadras por la Avenida Castilla para llegar al restaurante La Olla Vieja.

Al señor Flores: 9. _____ (Seguir) derecho hacia la Plaza Calderón y

10. _____ (buscar) la taquilla del Teatro Real.

SCORE [   ]

B. Ana and her family are touring Cuenca. Complete her conversation with a local resident. Use each expression once. (6 points)

perder	dónde queda	va mal	voy bien	disculpe	seguir derecho

ANA   Ehh... es difícil leer este mapa. Señora, 11. _____ . Estoy buscando un

lugar que no encuentro en mi mapa. ¿Sabe usted si 12. _____ para el

Museo Folklórico?

SEÑORA   No, me parece que usted 13. _____ . Para llegar al museo, hay que

tomar la calle Presidente Córdova y 14. _____ por cuatro cuadras.

ANA   ¿Y me puede decir 15. _____ el correo?

Alternative Quiz 9-1A

Señora Sí, está cerca del museo, en la Calle Gran Colombia. No se puede

16. _____ .

Ana Muchas gracias, señora.

SCORE [   ]

C. Look at the picture of the village of Molinos, then read the statements below. Write the name of the person or place described in each statement. (9 points)

_____ 17. Están delante del monumento de la plaza.

_____ 18. Está al lado de la panadería.

_____ 19. Se encuentra con un amigo cerca de la esquina de la casa.

_____ 20. Está detrás del árbol.

_____ 21. Se encuentra con un amigo delante de la tienda.

_____ 22. Está bajando por la calle hacia la plaza.

SCORE [   ]

TOTAL SCORE [   ] /30

Holt Spanish 2 ¡Ven conmigo!, Chapter 9

¡Día de mercado!

CAPÍTULO 9

■ SEGUNDO PASO

Maximum Score: 35

Grammar and Vocabulary

A. Cristóbal is shopping for clothes for his summer job. Complete his comments with the Spanish equivalents of the comparative expressions in parentheses. (12 points)

1. ¡Qué raro! Estos dos cinturones son de la misma talla pero el marrón es

   _____ el negro. *(longer than)*

2. Prefiero esta corbata. Es _____ las otras pero cuesta menos. *(as pretty as)*

3. La chaqueta de rayas me queda _____ la azul. *(tighter than)*

4. Estos pantalones me quedan _____ los otros. *(looser than)*

5. Mira... Este traje azul es _____ el gris. *(as expensive as)*

6. Estos zapatos negros son _____ los marrones. *(less comfortable than)*

7. ¡Nada de esta tienda me queda bien! La ropa aquí es para personas _____

   yo. *(thinner than)*

8. Vamos al Almacén Núñez. Los dependientes allí son _____ que éstos pero

   tienen mejores precios. *(less friendly)*

   SCORE [____]

B. Read the statements made by shoppers and employees at a department store. Write **C** if the statement was made by a **cliente** or **D** if it was made by a **dependiente**. (7 points)

_____ 9. ¿Dónde están los probadores?

_____ 10. Lo siento, ya no nos quedan más camisetas azules.

_____ 11. ¿Qué talla usa usted?

_____ 12. ¿Cómo le queda el vestido, señora?

_____ 13. ¿Me puedo probar estos pantalones?

_____ 14. Le queda un poco grande esa camisa. ¿Quiere probarse otra?

_____ 15. ¿Me puede atender, por favor?

SCORE [____]

Alternative Quiz 9-2A

C. Write the Spanish words for the indicated people and items in the store Novedades Alma.
(16 points)

16. _____

17. _____

18. _____

19. _____

20. _____

21. _____

22. _____

23. _____

SCORE ☐

TOTAL SCORE ☐ /35

Holt Spanish 2 ¡Ven conmigo!, Chapter 9

¡Día de mercado!

■ TERCER PASO

Maximum Score: 35

Grammar and Vocabulary

A. Diego is at an open-air market shopping for gifts. Put his conversation with the vendor in the correct order by lettering the statements from **a** to **i**. (18 points)

Vendedora

_____ 1. Muy bien, joven. ¡Pero recuerda que en los almacenes los precios son fijos!

_____ 2. Esa cartera cuesta mil doscientos pesos. Es de cuero muy fino.

_____ 3. Buenos días, joven. ¿Qué me compra? ¿Sandalias, carteras, cinturones?

_____ 4. Lo siento, pero no se la puedo dejar a ese precio. Se la doy por 850 pesos, pero es mi última oferta.

_____ 5. Pues, para usted le voy a rebajar el precio a mil pesos.

Diego

_____ 6. Gracias, pero no la compro. Creo que voy a mirar un poco más.

_____ 7. No sé... Todavía me parece caro. Le doy 700 pesos.

_____ 8. Buenos días, señora. Busco una cartera como regalo para mi papá. ¿Qué precio tiene esta cartera?

_____ 9. ¿Mil doscientos pesos? Me parece muy caro.

SCORE _____

B. Complete the statements and questions made by a shopper and salesperson with the correct word or expression. (9 points)

10. Perdón. ¿Qué precio _____ este suéter?
    a. tienen
    b. cuesta
    c. tiene

11. Esta semana, todos los suéteres de lana están _____ . Cuestan 900 pesos.
    a. en barata
    b. gratis
    c. a veinte por ciento

12. ¿Sólo 900 pesos? ¡Qué _____ ! Es un precio buenísimo.
    a. talla
    b. ganga
    c. caro

CAPÍTULO 9

Alternative Quiz 9-3A

13. Y si usted necesita camisas, hoy están _____ . Si compra una a 300 pesos, le regalamos la otra.
    a. a precios fijos
    b. a dos por una
    c. en el mercado al aire libre

14. No necesito camisas, pero sí me gusta esta chaqueta. ¿Me puede _____ el precio un poco?
    a. dejar
    b. regalar
    c. rebajar

15. Lo siento, pero es imposible. Para regatear hay que ir _____ .
    a. al mercado
    b. al probador
    c. al almacén

SCORE [____]

C. Angélica bought gifts at the market for her family. Explain which gift is for each person, using the information in her list. Include the correct direct object pronoun in your sentences. (8 points)

MODELO   ¿Para quién compró el cinturón?
         (Escribes) Lo compró para su papá.

> cinturón—papá
>
> sandalias—mamá
>
> sombrero—tío Eduardo
>
> blusa—abuela
>
> aretes—tía Azucena

16. ¿Para quién compró los aretes? _____

17. ¿Para quién compró la blusa? _____

18. ¿Para quién compró el sombrero? _____

19. ¿Para quién compró las sandalias? _____

SCORE [____]

TOTAL SCORE [____] /35

Holt Spanish 2 ¡Ven conmigo!, Chapter 9

¡Cuéntame!

■ PRIMER PASO

Maximum Score: 30

Grammar and Vocabulary

A. Carmen is describing a family wedding she went to last Saturday. Complete her description with the correct preterite form of the verbs in parentheses. Remember to use the correct reflexive pronoun. (10 points)

Mi primo Memo **1.** _____ (casarse) con su novia Carlota el sábado. Fue una

boda muy interesante. Primero, mi familia y yo llegamos tarde porque yo

2. _____ (perderse) buscando la iglesia. Luego, durante la ceremonia la mamá

de Carlota **3.** _____ (dormirse) porque estaba tan cansada. Después, en la

recepción, Memo le **4.** _____ (leer) un poema de amor a Carlota. Qué romántico,

¿no? Y también en la recepción, mi prima Claudia conoció a un amigo de Carlota y creo que los

dos **5.** _____ (enamorarse). ¿Qué más pasó? Mi tío Gregorio

6. _____ (caerse). Al principio todos los invitados **7.** _____

(creer) que se hizo daño, pero por suerte no le pasó nada serio. Pero sí

8. _____ (romperse) varios platos y vasos. Al final, a las dos de la mañana, los

novios **9.** _____ (despedirse) de los invitados. Para la luna de miel, ellos

10. _____ (irse) a la Florida.

SCORE _____

B. The students in Mrs. Marcos' class are all writing mystery stories. Below are beginnings to six stories. Complete each sentence with the correct imperfect and preterite forms of the verbs in parentheses. Read carefully to decide whether to use the preterite or the imperfect. (12 points)

11. _____ (Hacer) sol y había mucha gente en la calle el día en que Beatriz

_____ (perderse) para siempre en la capital.

12. _____ (Ser) las nueve de la noche cuando el detective Mora

_____ (llamar) a su cliente con unas noticias urgentes.

13. Don Francisco _____ (desayunar) tranquilamente cuando

_____ (recibir) dos llamadas telefónicas misteriosas.

◈ Alternative Quiz 10-1A

14. Cuando Berta _____ (ver) al hombre calvo por primera vez, recuerdo que

ella y yo _____ (ir) al parque.

15. El señor Rendón y su gato _____ (dormir) en el sofá cuando los dos

_____ (oír) algo en el patio.

16. La doctora Alvarado ya _____ (sentirse) preocupada cuando dos pacientes

más _____ (llegar) con los mismos síntomas raros.

SCORE [   ]

C. Look at the four photos, then match each one with the sentences that best describe the
weather in that photo. Some sentences may have more than one matching photo. (8 points)

a.

b.

c.

d.

_____ 17. ¡Qué húmedo está!

_____ 18. ¡Qué truenos tan fuertes! ¿Te
asustaste?

_____ 19. ¿Viste ese rayo? ¡Fue enorme!

_____ 20. Casi siempre cae un aguacero
por la tarde.

_____ 21. Está muy nublado hoy.

_____ 22. ¡Qué tormenta tan tremenda!

_____ 23. Me gusta la niebla.

_____ 24. Está despejado y hace calor.

SCORE [   ]

TOTAL SCORE [   ] /30

¡Cuéntame!

■ SEGUNDO PASO

Grammar and Vocabulary

A. Ignacio is writing his own version of *Beauty and the Beast*. Complete it with the correct preterite or imperfect form of the verbs in parentheses. (24 points)

Érase una vez, en un pueblo pequeño, una niña muy inteligente y valiente que se llam-

aba Bella. Ella y su familia **1.** _____ (ser) muy pobres. Un día, Bella

2. _____ (decidir) salir del pueblo a buscar su fortuna. Ella

3. _____ (irse) sin despedirse de nadie. Eran las once de la noche y todos

en la casa **4.** _____ (dormir) cuando Bella **5.** _____

(levantarse) e **6.** _____ (hacer) su maleta en silencio.

¡Qué frío **7.** _____ (hacer) y qué oscuro **8.** _____

(estar)! Bella caminaba tranquilamente por el camino cuando de repente

9. _____ (ver) un castillo enorme. Como Bella era tan valiente,

10. _____ (llegar) al castillo y **11.** _____ (llamar) a la

puerta. Después de unos minutos, la puerta **12.** _____ (abrirse) y...

SCORE _____

Alternative Quiz 10-2A

CAPÍTULO 10

B. Cristina is writing a story for her school's literary magazine. Next to each picture, write the Spanish words she needs to tell her story. (6 points)

13.  _____ 14.  _____

15.  _____ 16. _____

17.  _____ 18.  _____

SCORE [ ]

C. Cristina and her classmates have now finished the first drafts of their stories. Read these sentences from their drafts and identify each as a **continuation (C)** or **ending (E)**. (5 points)

_____ 19. De repente, todos oyeron a alguien que llamaba a la puerta.

_____ 20. Así que finalmente encontraron al ladrón y el dinero robado.

_____ 21. Entonces el rey fue a buscar el collar de oro.

_____ 22. Fue cuando llegó el enano con la carta.

_____ 23. Al final, se fueron todos a vivir en el castillo enorme.

SCORE [ ]

TOTAL SCORE [ ] /35

Holt Spanish 2 ¡Ven conmigo!, Chapter 10

CAPÍTULO

¡Cuéntame!

■ TERCER PASO

Maximum Score: 35

Grammar and Vocabulary

A. Juan is gossiping about why so few people showed up at the club meeting. Complete the explanations of why people didn't attend with the correct preterite form of **tener** and the expressions. (9 points)

1. Yo _____ que ir al entrenamiento *(practice)* de voleibol.

2. Creo que Inés y Julián _____ que ayudar en casa.

3. Graciela _____ que estudiar para el examen de química.

4. Y la profesora Montenegro _____ un problema con su carro.

5. Gabriela, tú _____ una cita con el dentista, ¿verdad?

6. Después, Andrés y yo _____ que hacer unos mandados.

SCORE [   ]

B. On your way to class, you overheard parts of different conversations. For each statement you overheard, decide if the speaker is **telling someone news (T)** or **reacting to news (R).** (12 points)

_____ 7. Fíjate, Jaime se va a vivir a otra ciudad.

_____ 8. No me lo creo. ¿Estás seguro?

_____ 9. ¿Tú crees? Personalmente, lo dudo.

_____ 10. ¡No me digas! ¿Qué pasó? ¡Cuéntame!

_____ 11. ¿Un OVNI en la cancha de fútbol? ¡No puede ser!

_____ 12. Oí que un grupo latino va a tocar en el baile.

_____ 13. ¿Te enteraste del problema en el laboratorio?

_____ 14. No vas a creer lo que le pasó a Daniela.

SCORE [   ]

CAPÍTULO 10

Alternative Quiz 10-3A

C. Noel is writing a letter to a friend who recently moved to another town. Complete his letter about all the latest news with the missing expressions. Use each expression once. (14 points)

hicieron las paces	noticias	chisme	metiche
	chismosos	furioso	rompieron

Ahora te cuento el **15.** _____ sobre Dolores y Jorge.

La semana pasada se pelearon y **16.** _____ . Parece que

Beto estaba **17.** _____ con Dolores. Dijo *(He said)* que

los amigos de ella eran todos unos **18.** _____ que se lo

pasaban hablando de la vida personal de los demás. ¡Fíjate! Pero ahora las últi-

mas **19.** _____ son que otra vez están juntos. Su amiga

Elena, que es una **20.** _____ , habló con los dos.

Entonces José llamó a Dolores y por fin **21.** _____ . Y no

vas a creer lo que le pasó a...

SCORE [   ]

TOTAL SCORE [/35]

CAPÍTULO 10

CAPÍTULO 11

Nuestro medio ambiente

■ PRIMER PASO

Grammar and Vocabulary

A. Respond to each question about the environment with a negative answer. Include the negative word that corresponds to the word underlined in the question. Remember that Spanish may use more than one negative word or expression in a sentence. (6 points)

1. En tu opinión, ¿alguien está preocupado por la situación?

   _____

2. ¿Tus amigos siempre tratan de reciclar *(to recycle)?*

   _____

3. En tu opinión, ¿hay una solución al problema del smog?

   _____

4. Entonces, ¿podemos hacer algo por las playas contaminadas?

   _____

   SCORE [   ]

B. Everyone in the Ecology Club has opinions about environmental issues. Use the words below to complete what club members say. (12 points)

desperdicio	combustibles	químicos	destrucción		
contaminación		selvas	tira		capa

ISABEL   A mí me parece muy serio la **5.** _____ del aire y del mar.

Cada vez más la gente **6.** _____ plástico y

7. _____ en los ríos y en las playas.

GRACIELA   ¿Leyeron ustedes el artículo sobre el Amazonas? ¡Es terrible! Estoy muy preocupada por las **8.** _____ tropicales.

LORENZO   Sí, eso y la **9.** _____ de la **10.** _____

de ozono son los problemas más graves.

CAPÍTULO 11

Alternative Quiz 11-1A

LUIS   Creo que otro problema es el **11.** _____ de los recursos na-

turales, como el petróleo, el aceite y otros **12.** _____ .

SCORE [   ]

C. You're preparing to appear on a quiz show on nature. Write the Spanish name for the animals described below. (12 points)

_____ 13. los mosquitos y las cucarachas son dos ejemplos de estos animales pequeños

_____ 14. un mamífero pequeño que sale de noche

_____ 15. una ave muy grande, en peligro de extinción, que vive en California y los Andes

_____ 16. un mamífero acuático muy grande

_____ 17. el ave que es símbolo de los Estados Unidos

_____ 18. un mamífero *(mammal)* acuático muy inteligente

a. los insectos

b. el delfín

c. el águila

d. el cóndor

e. el murciélago

f. la ballena

SCORE [   ]

TOTAL SCORE [/30]

Holt Spanish 2 ¡Ven conmigo!, Chapter 11

CAPÍTULO 11

CAPÍTULO

11

Nuestro medio ambiente

■ SEGUNDO PASO

Grammar and Vocabulary

A. Read the short articles about several animals, then write the name of the animal referred to in the statements that follow. (14 points)

Los osos pardos. Por mucho tiempo habitaron la Península Ibérica de norte a sur. Hoy, apenas quedan cien osos pardos en la península. Por eso, la especie está en peligro de extinción pese a los esfuerzos por salvarla.

Las tortugas marinas. Este hermoso animal marino puede desaparecer de la tierra. El hombre es el culpable de esta tragedia ya que las compañías industriales de comida están destruyendo su medio ambiente.

Los delfines. En las costas peruanas, se pesca indiscriminadamente a estos animales. La pobreza es la causa de ello: la pesca del delfín es un modo de asegurar el bienestar familiar. Por lo tanto es urgente hacer algo acerca de la pobreza.

El águila calva. Ella es el símbolo nacional de los Estados Unidos. Por un tiempo, estuvo a punto de desaparecer, por hoy continúa habitando los cielos y los bosques de este país.

_____ 1. At one point, this animal was in danger of becoming extinct.

_____ 2. There are only about 100 of these animals left.

_____ 3. This animal is making a comeback in its former habitat.

_____ 4. This species is endangered despite efforts to save it.

_____ 5. Fishing these animals is a way for poor people to make a living.

_____ 6. The food industry is reponsible for making this animal an endangered species.

_____ 7. These animals are being fished off the coast of Peru.

SCORE _____

CAPÍTULO 11

Alternative Quiz 11-2A

B. Some friends are talking about ecological problems and their conse-
quences. Complete their conversation with an appropriate expression
from the box. Use each expression at least once. (9 points)

por consiguiente
por lo tanto   por eso

LUISA   Las fábricas tiran químicos en los ríos y **8.** _____ los ríos,
lagos y mares están contaminados.

MARIO   Hay muchos automóviles y autobuses en la ciudad y **9.** _____
hay demasiado ruido.

SUSANA   También hay gente que no usa el sistema de transporte público;

10. _____ el smog está cada vez peor.

MIGUEL   Muchas personas no quieren reciclar *(to recycle)*; **11.** _____ ,
hay mucha basura.

BLANCA   Muchos creen que el gobierno debe hacer algo; **12.** _____
no quieren hacer nada como individuos.

ISABEL   Los mares están muy contaminados y **13.** _____ muchas
especies de peces están en peligro de extinción.

SCORE [   ]

C. Sometimes Manuel agrees with Juanita's opinions about environmental problems, and sometimes he doesn't. Read Juanita's statements, then choose the response that best indicates
Manuel's agreement or disagreement, according to the cues. (12 points)

_____ **14.** Todos tenemos que ser más responsables y cuidar más el medio ambiente.
(Manuel agrees.)
   a. ¡Eso es!   **b.** Mira, no lo creo.

_____ **15.** La destrucción de las selvas tropicales es una tragedia. *(Manuel agrees.)*
   a. No estoy de acuerdo.   **b.** Tienes razón.

_____ **16.** El problema de la capa de ozono es muy grave, ¿no crees? *(Manuel disagrees.)*
   a. Me parece que no.   **b.** ¡Claro que sí!

_____ **17.** Si no dejamos de desperdiciar recursos como el agua y el petróleo, vamos a
enfrentar una crisis. *(Manuel agrees.)*
   a. Así es la cosa.   **b.** ¡Al contrario!

_____ **18.** No hay suficiente transporte público. Por eso, hay mucha contaminación del aire.
(Manuel agrees.)
   a. ¡Te equivocas!   **b.** Sin duda alguna.

_____ **19.** Hay muchos animales en peligro de extinción. ¡Es urgente hacer algo!
(Manuel disagrees.)
   a. Estoy de acuerdo.   **b.** No me parece.

SCORE [   ]

TOTAL SCORE [   ] /35

CAPÍTULO

11 Nuestro medio ambiente

■ TERCER PASO

Maximum Score: 35

Grammar and Vocabulary

A. Complete the poster the Ecology Club made for "Save Our Planet" week with the missing verbs. Use each verb only once. (15 points)

| desesperarse | apagar | conservar | reciclar | tirar |
| mantener | resolver | cambiar | evitar | proteger |

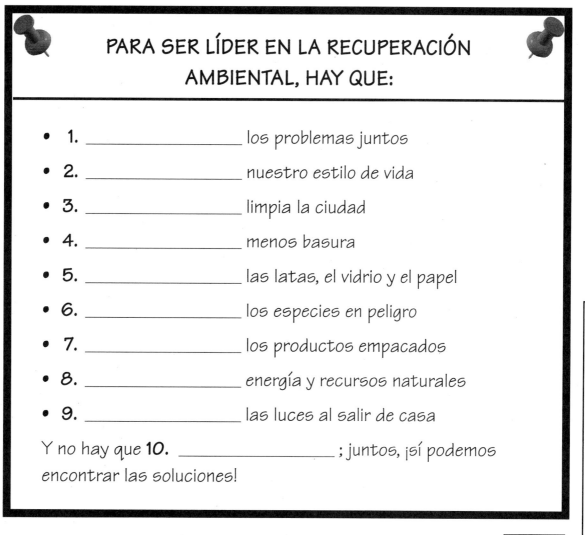

PARA SER LÍDER EN LA RECUPERACIÓN
AMBIENTAL, HAY QUE:

- 1. _____ los problemas juntos

- 2. _____ nuestro estilo de vida

- 3. _____ limpia la ciudad

- 4. _____ menos basura

- 5. _____ las latas, el vidrio y el papel

- 6. _____ los especies en peligro

- 7. _____ los productos empacados

- 8. _____ energía y recursos naturales

- 9. _____ las luces al salir de casa

Y no hay que **10.** _____ ; juntos, ¡sí podemos encontrar las soluciones!

SCORE [   ]

CAPÍTULO 11

Alternative Quiz 11-3A

B. Marisol has some ideas for the Ecology Club's next environmental awareness campaign. Complete the suggestions she makes to other members with the **nosotros** commands of the verbs in parentheses. (10 points)

11. _____ (Ir) a la oficina del director para explicarle nuestras ideas.

12. _____ (Desfilar) por el centro en bicicletas y carros eléctricos

13. _____ (Hacer) un concurso *(contest)* de reciclaje.

14. _____ (Organizar) una reunión con otros grupos ambientales.

15. _____ (Escribir) cartas al presidente y al congreso.

SCORE [   ]

C. Pablo is predicting what will happen to the environment if certain problems aren't addressed. Write his predictions by combining the expressions given with **si**. (10 points)

MODELO no hacer nada/enfrentar una crisis
        Si no hacemos nada, vamos a enfrentar una crisis.

16. trabajar juntos/resolver los problemas

_____

17. comprar menos productos empacados/tener menos basura

_____

18. no cuidar las especies/desaparecer

_____

19. usar menos los carros/tener menos smog

_____

20. no dejar de contaminar los lagos y ríos/no tener agua limpia

_____

SCORE [   ]

TOTAL SCORE [/35]

Holt Spanish 2 ¡Ven conmigo!, Chapter 11

CAPÍTULO 12

Veranos pasados, veranos por venir

Alternative Quiz 12-1A

▪ PRIMER PASO

Maximum Score: 35

Grammar and Vocabulary

A. Marta visited relatives in Puerto Rico this summer, and is now back home. Complete her letter to her cousin Pedro with the missing expressions. (9 points)

> siguen   cariño   dale un saludo   te echo
> abrazo   Querido   gracias por   sabías que   noticias

1. _____ Pedro,

¿Cómo estás? Ya llegó tu carta, y **2.** _____ las fotos que me mandaste de las

vacaciones en Puerto Rico. Están en mi cuarto y las miro cada vez que **3.** _____

de menos. Por cierto, (By the way) ¿**4.** _____ pienso jugar en el equipo de voleibol

del colegio este año? ¿Tu amigo Rafael y tú **5.** _____ jugando al voleibol todos

los días? ¿Y cómo está Rafael? Por favor, **6.** _____ de mi parte. Bueno, me

despido porque no tengo más **7.** _____ y porque tengo que ayudar a mamá. Les

mando un **8.** _____ a todos, especialmente a ti y a la tía Rosario.

Con **9.** _____ ,

Marta

SCORE [   ]

B. Read the statements about what people plan or would like to do this summer. Then write sentences explaining what each person should do. Use each of the listed expressions only once. (12 points)

> hacerse amigo/a de...   quedarse en un albergue juvenil   encontrar un empleo
> montar en tabla de vela   quedarse con sus parientes   quedarse en casa

10. Ricardo y Roberto necesitan dinero para pagar un viaje en bicicleta.

_____

11. Mercedes tiene ganas de aprender un deporte nuevo e interesante este verano.

_____

Alternative Quiz 12-1A

12. Sebastián se mudó *(moved)* aquí en mayo, y le gustaría conocer a más gente.

_____

13. A Nora le encantaría ver a sus primos en Santo Domingo.

_____

14. Santiago y yo queremos viajar a México, pero no tenemos mucho dinero.

_____

15. Natalia no quiere hacer nada—¡sólo quiere descansar!

_____

SCORE [   ]

C. It's the first day back at school, and everyone's talking about summer vacation. Complete the sentences with the preterite of the verbs in parentheses. (14 points)

16. Tomás, tú _____ aquí en casa, ¿verdad? ¿ _____ un empleo? (quedarse, encontrar)

17. Alberto _____ a San Diego. Allí _____ a un curso de verano sobre el medio ambiente. (ir, asistir)

18. Sergio _____ un viaje a México y _____ muchos regalos para sus amigos. (hacer, comprar)

19. Pilar y yo _____ en un maratón. Nosotros _____ casi todo el verano haciendo entrenamiento. (correr, pasar)

20. Rosa y Fernanda _____ en un parque nacional y _____ amigas de mucha gente en el camping. (acampar, hacerse)

21. Paloma y su familia _____ a Guatemala y _____ unas pirámides. (viajar, escalar)

22. Luego, en agosto yo _____ a la costa a la casa de mis tíos. Allí _____ a bucear. (ir, aprender)

SCORE [   ]

TOTAL SCORE [   ] /35

CAPÍTULO 12

Veranos pasados, veranos por venir

Alternative Quiz 12-2A

Maximum Score: 30

■ SEGUNDO PASO

Grammar and Vocabulary

A. Benjamín went to visit some cousins on their ranch near San Antonio, Texas. Use the missing expressions to complete his descripton of his experiences there. (8 points)

> seco   quedé impresionado   clima   está rodeado
> buena gente   lindísimo   nos llevamos   bastante

Lo pasé muy bien en el rancho de mis tíos. Mis primos Benito y Rosario son muy

1. _____ . Nosotros 2. _____ muy bien, y espero ir

a visitarlos el próximo verano también. ¡El rancho es 3. _____ ! Yo

4. _____ con todo lo que vi. El rancho 5. _____ de

colinas, y muy cerca hay arroyos *(creeks)* y lagos pequeños. En el verano, como el

6. _____ allí es muy 7. _____ , a veces no hay

mucha agua en los ríos y lagos. Pero esta vez sí, y como hace 8. _____

calor allí, fuimos a nadar casi todos los días.

SCORE [____]

B. You and your classmates met a lot of people on the class trip. Complete the sentences about how everyone felt about their new acquaintances. Use the correct pronoun and preterite form of **caer.** (10 points)

9. Parece que a Andrés _____ _____ mal el conductor del autobús.

10. Alejandro, ¿a ti cómo _____ _____ los turistas italianos?

11. A mí _____ _____ bien nuestro guía. Era un tipazo.

12. La directora del museo estuvo muy antipática con nuestro grupo. Creo que nosotros

_____ _____ mal a ella.

13. Quería hacerme amiga de unos turistas alemanes, pero no pude. Creo que yo

_____ _____ mal a ellos.

SCORE [____]

Alternative Quiz 12-2A

CAPÍTULO 12

C. Antonio is describing his best friend from childhood. Complete part of his description with the imperfect form of the verbs in parentheses. (12 points)

Mi perro Oso fue mi primer mejor amigo. Mis padres lo compraron cuando yo

14. _____ (tener) tres años. Lo cierto es que ese perro y yo

15. _____ (llevarse) muy bien. Nosotros 16. _____ (ser)

como hermanos. Oso 17. _____ (dormir) en mi cuarto y todos los días él y yo

18. _____ (despertarse) temprano para ir al campo a jugar. A Oso le

19. _____ (encantar) hacer travesuras y pelearse con los gatos del barrio.

Mamá y papá siempre 20. _____ (decir) que Oso me

21. _____ (cuidar) mejor que una niñera *(babysitter)*. Recuerdo una vez...

SCORE _____

TOTAL SCORE _____ /30

Holt Spanish 2 ¡Ven conmigo!, Chapter 12

12 Veranos pasados, veranos por venir

Alternative Quiz 12-3A

Maximum Score: 35

■ TERCER PASO

Grammar and Vocabulary

A. Imagine that today is Wednesday the 7th. Look over part of Sara's calendar, then indicate **cierto** or **falso** for each statement that follows. (14 points)

lunes	martes	miércoles	jueves	viernes	sábado	domingo
5	6 examen de química	⑦ ayudar a mamá en la tienda	8	9 dentista—cita 4:00	10	11
12	13	14 Susana—aeropuerto 3:56	15 cenar con Carlos	16	17 hacer planes—fiesta de la abuela	18

_____ 1. Llega su amiga el día anterior a la cena con Carlos.

_____ 2. Para fines de este mes, ella piensa organizar la fiesta para su abuela.

_____ 3. La semana que viene llega su amiga Susana para una visita.

_____ 4. Dentro de dos días, va a ver a su amigo Carlos.

_____ 5. Cuando vuelva a casa hoy, Sara tiene que trabajar.

_____ 6. Pronto Sara tiene un examen de química.

_____ 7. Sara necesita ir al dentista inmediatamente.

SCORE [   ]

B. Teresa is talking about everyone's plans for the near and more distant future. Combine the expressions and write sentences explaining what will happen when the following events take place. Remember that the subjunctive is used after **cuando** when talking about events in the indefinite future. (12 points)

MODELO Cuando vuelva a casa esta tarde/yo/estudiar mucho
        (Escribes) Cuando vuelva a casa esta tarde, voy a estudiar mucho.

8. Cuando terminen las clases/yo/descansar mucho

_____ .

CAPÍTULO 12

Alternative Quiz 12-3A

9. Cuando ella tenga más dinero/mi hermana mayor/comprar un carro

_____ .

10. Cuando vuelva al colegio en septiembre/yo/tomar muchas clases difíciles

_____ .

11. Cuando ella tenga tiempo/mi amiga Verónica/visitarme

_____ .

12. Cuando lleguen mis primos/nosotros/divertirnos mucho

_____ .

13. Cuando encuentre un empleo/yo/comprar una computadora

_____ .

SCORE [   ]

C. Cristóbal is on vacation in San Diego. Combine the correct form of **ir + a** with the infinitives in parentheses to complete his postcard to a friend. (9 points)

Hola Diego,

Aquí estoy en San Diego, pasándolo fenomenal. El viernes mi hermana y yo

14. _____ (ir) al zoológico famoso. Si hay tiempo, ella tam-

bién 15. _____ (visitar) el campus de la Universidad de San

Diego. Mañana yo 16. _____ (tomar) una clase de tabla de

vela en la playa. Ya te mandé unas fotos de mi excursión al parque Mission Bay que tú

17. _____ (recibir) pronto. Y tú, ¿qué tal? ¿Qué

18. _____ (hacer) en agosto? Darío y Eduardo

19. _____ (quedarse) conmigo por dos semanas—¿quieres

venir también? Te escribo más tarde.

Chao,
Cristóbal

SCORE [   ]

TOTAL SCORE [   ] /35

Answer Key

Answers to Alternative Quizzes 1-1A, 1-2A, and 1-3A

Alternative Quiz 1-1A

A. (8 points: 1 point per item)
1. diecinueve, once
2. treinta y cuatro, ochenta y tres
3. quince
4. sesenta, veintidós
5. doce

B. (12 points: 1.5 points per item)
6. venezolanos
7. costarricense
8. guatemalteca
9. hondureños
10. uruguayas
11. puertorriqueños
12. peruano
13. española

C. (5 points: 1 point per item)
14. tengo
15. tienen
16. tenemos
17. tiene
18. tienes

D. (10 points: 1 point per item)
19. atléticos; cómicos
20. pelirrojas; jóvenes
21. canoso; inteligente
22. trabajadora; simpática
23. altos; leales

Alternative Quiz 1-2A

A. (10 points: 2 points per item)
1. Hortensia sale a las nueve de la mañana. Va a nadar.
2. Julio y Rubén salen a las diez de la mañana. Van a asistir al partido.
3. Yo salgo a las doce y media de la tarde. Voy a ir al centro comercial.
4. Tú sales a las cuatro de la tarde. Vas a correr en el parque.
5. Mis amigos y yo salimos a las siete de la noche. Vamos a ver una película.

B. (10 points: 1 point per item)
6. mirar
7. corren
8. descansan
9. pasamos
10. toca
11. recibo
12. busco
13. abro
14. vive
15. debo

C. (15 points: 1.5 points per item)
16. vienes
17. voy
18. cuido
19. haces
20. asistimos
21. comemos
22. Saco
23. corto
24. regresamos
25. preparamos

Alternative Quiz 1-3A

A. (6 points: 1 point per item)
1. c
2. a
3. b
4. c
5. a
6. c

B. (12 points: 1.5 points per item)
7. les
8. le
9. me
10. te
11. nos
12. me
13. nos
14. te

C. (12 points: 2 points per item)
15. me; encantan/gustan
16. le; encantan/gustan
17. les; choca
18. les; chocan
19. nos; gustan
20. le; gustan

Answers to Alternative Quizzes 2-1A, 2-2A, and 2-3A

Alternative Quiz 2-1A

A. (10 points: 2 point per item)
1. nos sentimos nerviosos
2. se sienten preocupados
3. te sientes emocionada
4. me siento feliz
5. se siente cansada

B. (7 points: 1 point per item)
6. estoy
7. están
8. están
9. está
10. estamos
11. estar
12. está

C. (8 points: 1 point per item)
13. e
14. c
15. g
16. a
17. f
18. b
19. d
20. h

D. (10 points: 2 points per item)
21. está deprimido
22. están de buen humor/emocionados
23. está de mal humor
24. está emocionada/de buen humor
25. estamos tranquilos

Alternative Quiz 2-2A

A. (9 points: 1.5 points per item)
1. preparé
2. bailó
3. nadaron
4. escuchamos
5. jugamos
6. sacaron

B. (10 points: 2 points per item)
7. hoy
8. ayer
9. la semana pasada
10. anoche
11. anteayer

C. (6 points: 1 point per item)
12. quieres
13. puedo
14. quiere
15. quiero
16. puedes
17. Podemos

D. (5 points: 1 point each)
18. Mi hermano y yo fuimos a la tienda de ropa.
19. Mis padres fueron al banco.
20. Mi hermano fue a la agencia de viajes.
21. Mamá y yo fuimos al almacén.
22. Yo fui a la librería.

Alternative Quiz 2-3A

A. (9 points: 1.5 points per item)
1. al lado
2. cerca
3. lejos
4. lejos
5. debajo
6. encima

B. (10 points: 2 points per item)
7. el océano
8. el edificio
9. el centro
10. la montaña
11. el rascacielos

C. (8 points: 2 points per item)
Answers will vary.

D. (8 points: 2 points per item)
Answers will vary. Possible answers:
16. Hace sol y hace mucho calor.
17. Hace buen tiempo. Hace sol.
18. Está lloviendo y hace viento.
19. Hace frío y está nevando.

CAPÍTULO 2

Holt Spanish 2 ¡Ven conmigo!, Chapter 2

Answers to Alternative Quizzes 3-1A, 3-2A, and 3-3A

Alternative Quiz 3-1A

A. (5 points: 1 point per item)
1. lentamente
2. inmediatamente
3. generalmente
4. rápidamente
5. típicamente

B. (6 points)
6. champú
7. un despertador
8. un espejo
9. un peine
10. un cepillo de dientes
11. pasta de dientes

C. (14 points: 2 points per item)
12. nos despertamos
13. ducharme
14. me afeito
15. me cepillo los dientes
16. se levanta
17. Se secan el pelo
18. se miran en el espejo

D. (5 points: 1 point per item)
19. se visten
20. me visto
21. se viste
22. nos vestimos
23. te vistes

Alternative Quiz 3-2A

A. (10 points: 2 points per item)
Answers will vary. Possible answers:
1. Las voy a tender ahora mismo.
2. Voy a regarlas el domingo.
3. Lo voy a limpiar el lunes.
4. Voy a lavarlos después de cenar.
5. La voy a pasar el sábado.

B. (8 points: 1 point per item)
6. ordenar
7. tender
8. el cuarto de baño
9. el césped
10. el polvo
11. barrer
12. quitar
13. regar

C. (10 points: 2 points per item)
14. Las limpió Manuel.
15. Lo preparó Rodolfo.
16. Los ordenaron Imelda, Rodolfo y Manuel.
17. Lo cortó Imelda.
18. Lo barrieron Imelda y Rodolfo.

D. (7 points: 1 point per item)
19. le toca
20. le toca
21. te toca
22. Te toca
23. me toca
24. me toca
25. me toca

Alternative Quiz 3-3A

A. (12 points: 1.5 points per item)
1. Usa la computadora.
2. Hace monopatín.
3. Bucea y nada.
4. Juegan en un equipo de voleibol.
5. Colecciona estampillas.
6. Trabajan en mecánica.
7. Se reúne con amigos.
8. Tocamos con la banda.

B. (8 points: 1 point per item)
9. Joel
10. Azucena
11. Azucena
12. Joel
13. Azucena y Joel
14. Azucena
15. Joel
16. Azucena

C. (10 points: 2 points per item)
17. Hace cuatro años que Ángel juega videojuegos.
18. Hace un año que Ricardo bucea.
19. Hace dos años que Fermín y Dolores tocan con la banda.
20. Hace siete meses que Inés hace monopatín.
21. Hace tres años que Dolores colecciona monedas.

D. (5 points: 1 point per item)
22. cuánto tiempo hace que
23. pasatiempos
24. Te interesan
25. estás loca por
26. empezaste/comenzaste

Answers to Alternative Quizzes 4-1A, 4-2A, and 4-3A

Alternative Quiz 4-1A

A. (4 points: 1 point per item)
1. No, no deberías preocuparte cuando cometes errores.
2. Sí, deberías hacer muchas preguntas en clase.
3. Sí, deberías estudiar todas las noches.
4. No, no deberías hacer la tarea con tus amigos por correo electrónico.

B. (7 points: 1 point per item)
5. tu opinión
6. creo que
7. para mí
8. mi opinión
9. crees que
10. Qué te parece
11. me parece

C. (12 points: 1.5 points per item)
12. sacar
13. repasar
14. de memoria
15. hacer
16. apuntes
17. hacer/entregar
18. seguir
19. cometer

D. (12 points: 1.5 points per item)
20. me preocupo
21. prestan
22. aprueban
23. copian
24. suspender
25. olvida
26. deja
27. pierde

Alternative Quiz 4-2A

A. (15 points: 1.5 points per item)
1. es
2. está
3. es
4. está
5. son
6. Es
7. está
8. está
9. Es
10. estamos

B. (7 points: 1 point per item)
11. conocen
12. conoce a
13. conoce
14. conocemos
15. conocer a
16. conozco a
17. conoces a

C. (8 points: 1 point per item)
18. Leo y Nuria son flojos.
19. Los estudiantes son generosos.
20. El sargento es exigente.
21. Antonio es aplicado.
22. María Elena es creativa.
23. Alicia es responsable.
24. Los muchachos son entusiastas.
25. Carlos es torpe.

Alternative Quiz 4-3A

A. (8 points: 2 points per item)
Answers will vary. Possible answers:
1. Berta los va a invitar.
2. Voy a llamarlo ahora mismo.
3. Sí, me llamó anoche.
4. Sí, voy a llamarte a las cuatro.

B. (8 points: 2 points per item)
5. Lo tomé a las seis.
6. La hermana de Lucila la recomendó.
7. Francisco y Guillermo los compraron.
8. Todos nosotros la pagamos.

C. (12 points: 1.5 points each)
9. platicaron
10. hicieron
11. tomó
12. se reunió
13. merendaron
14. miraron
15. fue
16. hizo

D. (7 points: 1 point per item)
17. b   21. b
18. b   22. b
19. a   23. a
20. b

CAPÍTULO 4

154 Student Make-Up Assignments

Holt Spanish 2 ¡Ven conmigo!, Chapter 4

Answers to Alternative Quizzes 5-1A, 5-2A, and 5-3A

Alternative Quiz 5-1A

A. (5 points: 1 point per item)
1. dieron
2. dio
3. dimos
4. di
5. Diste

B. (12 points: 1 point per item)
6. corrí; corrieron; corrió
7. asistieron; asistí; asistió
8. comí; comió; comieron
9. se inscribió; me inscribí; se inscribieron

C. (8 points: 1 point per item)
10. h or g
11. f
12. d
13. c
14. a
15. g or h
16. b
17. e

D. (5 points: 1 point per item)
18. dormimos
19. durmieron
20. dormiste
21. durmió
22. dormí

Alternative Quiz 5-2A

A. (15 points: 1.5 points per item)
1. digas
2. seas
3. juegues
4. estés
5. añadas
6. fumes
7. comas
8. compres
9. vayas
10. busques

B. (5 points: 1 point per item)
11. el estrés
12. entrenarse
13. relajarse

14. hacer régimen
15. las grasas

C. (15 points: 1.5 points each)
16. Sal
17. Di
18. Ten
19. Salta
20. Ve
21. Come
22. Evita
23. Corre
24. Respira
25. Haz

Alternative Quiz 5-3A

A. (9 points: 1.5 points per item)
1. pude
2. pudiste
3. pudo
4. pudimos
5. pudieron
6. pudo

B. (12 points: 1.5 points each)
7. el cuello
8. el codo
9. el muslo
10. la rodilla
11. el tobillo
12. la pantorrilla
13. la muñeca
14. el hombro

C. (8 points: 2 points per item)
15. se lastimó la muñeca
16. se torcieron el tobillo
17. se hizo daño a la rodilla
18. tiene calambre en el hombro

D. (6 points: 1 point each)
19. se enfermó
20. nos cansamos
21. se olvidó
22. se quejó
23. me acordé
24. se divirtió

Answers to Alternative Quizzes 6-1A, 6-2A, and 6-3A

Alternative Quiz 6-1A

A. (5 points: 1 point per item)
1. sé
2. sabemos
3. sabe
4. saben
5. Sabes

B. (12 points: 1.5 points per item)
6. sabe
7. sabemos
8. conoce a
9. conoce a
10. sabe
11. sé
12. saber
13. conozco

C. (12 points: 1.5 points per item)
14. boda
15. iglesia
16. lancha
17. turistas
18. guía
19. edificios
20. autobuses
21. conductores

D. (6 points: 1 point per item)
22. disculpe
23. Me podría decir
24. por supuesto
25. sabe
26. no estoy seguro
27. no tengo ni idea

Alternative Quiz 6-2A

A. (12 points: 1.5 points per item)
1. boletos
2. estación
3. taquilla
4. ida y vuelta
5. maletero
6. andén
7. vía
8. pasajeros

B. (8 points: 1 point per item)
9. hicimos
10. visitamos
11. nos subimos
12. exploraron
13. encantó
14. decidió
15. sacó
16. vio

C. (10 points: 2 points per item)
Answers to 18–20 will vary on the phrase. Possible answers:
17. Para empezar; escribió
18. Luego; se reunió
19. Después; fue
20. A continuación; comió
21. Por último; se subió

Alternative Quiz 6-3A

A. (10 points: 2 points per item)
Answers will vary. Possible answers:
1. Para mí, un agua mineral.
2. ¿Está la sopa muy picante?
3. ¿Qué me recomienda?
4. De postre, me trae un flan, por favor.
5. Me trae la cuenta, por favor.

B. (6 points: 1 point per item)
6. A los señores Ramos
7. El señor Méndez
8. Los señores Ruiz
9. siete
10. Sergio, Tomás, Alberto
11. Tomás

C. (12 points: 1.5 points per item)
12. pidió
13. sirvieron
14. pedí
15. sirvió
16. pidieron
17. sirvió
18. pedimos
19. sirvieron

D. (7 points: 1 point per item)
20. trajo
21. trajiste
22. traje
23. traje
24. trajo
25. trajimos
26. trajo

Holt Spanish 2 ¡Ven conmigo!, Chapter 6

CAPÍTULO 6

Answers to Alternative Quizzes 7-1A, 7-2A, and 7-3A

Alternative Quiz 7-1A

A. (5 points: 1 point per item)
1. iban
2. iba
3. iba
4. íbamos
5. ibas

B. (11 points: 1 point per item)
6. vivíamos
7. tenían
8. ayudábamos
9. gustaba
10. venían
11. trabajaban
12. sabía
13. cocinábamos
14. lavaba
15. prefería
16. servían

C. (5 points: 1 point per item)
17. veíamos
18. veía
19. veía
20. veían
21. veías

D. (14 points: 2 points per item)
Answers will vary. Possible answers:
22. compartíamos helados y dulces
23. se asustaba
24. soñaba con jugar al béisbol
25. peleaban
26. contaban chistes
27. construía casas
28. hacía travesuras

Alternative Quiz 7-2A

A. (8 points: 1 point per item)
1. u   5. o
2. y   6. e
3. y   7. o
4. e   8. e

B. (14 points: 2 points per item)
9. Manuel era solitario.
10. Mi primo Luis era aventurero.
11. Mis amigos y yo éramos conversadores.

12. Mi hermano Mario era bondadoso.
13. Mi prima Ana era egoísta.
14. Mis hermanas menores eran consentidas.
15. Yo era impaciente.

C. (8 points: 1 point per item)
16. había
17. había
18. hay
19. hay
20. había
21. hay
22. hay
23. había

Alternative Quiz 7-3A

A. (9 points: 1.5 points per item)
1. b   4. e
2. c   5. f
3. a   6. d

B. (12 points: 2 points per item)
7. Los profesores aquí son tan exigentes como los de Nueva York.
8. Los exámenes aquí son tan difíciles como los de Nueva York.
9. Los estudiantes aquí son tan aplicados como los de Nueva York.
10. La cafetería aquí es tan horrible como la de Nueva York.
11. Las clases aquí son tan interesantes como las de Nueva York.
12. El director aquí es tan justo como el de Nueva York.

C. (14 points: 2 points per item)
13. Azucena sacaba tantas notas altas como Ricardo.
14. Azucena tocaba tantos instrumentos musicales como Ricardo.
15. Azucena iba a tantas fiestas como Ricardo.
16. Azucena practicaba tantos deportes como Ricardo.
17. Azucena tenía tanta tarea como Ricardo.
18. Azucena leía tantos libros como Ricardo.
19. Azucena estudiaba tantas horas al día como Ricardo.

Answers to Alternative Quizzes 8-1A, 8-2A, and 8-3A

Alternative Quiz 8-1A

A. (11 points: 1 point per item)
1. d
2. i
3. a
4. g
5. f
6. c
7. e
8. j
9. h
10. k
11. b

B. (12 points: 1.5 points per item)
12. ocupadísimo
13. riquísimas
14. larguísimo
15. carísimo
16. buenísima
17. tristísima
18. aburridísima
19. divertidísima

C. (7 points: 1 point per item)
20. Los monos más traviesos de todos son los pequeños.
21. El loro más inteligente de todo el zoológico es de Guatemala.
22. El animal más feo de todos es el cocodrilo.
23. El actor más guapo de todos es el nuevo actor cubano.
24. La cola más larga del parque de atracciones es para los carros chocones.
25. Los efectos especiales más creativos del festival son los de *Galaxias 2050*.
26. La atracción más aburrida del parque de atracciones es la rueda de Chicago.

D. (5 points: 1 point per item)
27. el mejor
28. las mejores
29. la peor
30. los peores
31. el mejor

Alternative Quiz 8-2A

A. (8 points: 1 point per item)
1. veías; estábamos
2. iban; compraba
3. regaba; daba
4. llevaba; hacíamos

B. (9 points: 1.5 points per item)
5. e
6. d
7. b
8. c
9. f
10. a

C. (18 points: 1.5 points per item)
11. a
12. con
13. que
14. X
15. X
16. de
17. a
18. en
19. a
20. por
21. de
22. X

Alternative Quiz 8-3A

A. (10 points: 1 point per item)
1. dijiste; parecía
2. dije; gustaba
3. dijimos; encantaban
4. dijeron; gustaban
5. dijo; parecían

B. (12 points: 1.5 point per item)
6. c
7. a
8. e
9. g
10. h
11. d
12. b
13. f

C. (8 points: 1 point per item)
14. dije
15. dijo
16. dijo
17. dijeron
18. dijiste
19. dijo
20. dijeron
21. dijimos

Holt Spanish 2 ¡Ven conmigo!, Chapter 8

CAPÍTULO 8

Answers to Alternative Quizzes 9-1A, 9-2A, and 9-3A

Alternative Quiz 9-1A

A. (15 points: 1.5 points per item)
1. Levántese
2. haga
3. se olvide
4. Empiecen
5. crucen
6. vayan
7. Dé
8. Bajen
9. Siga
10. busque

B. (6 points: 1 point per item)
11. disculpe
12. voy bien
13. va mal
14. seguir derecho
15. dónde queda
16. perder

C. (9 points: 1.5 points per item)
Some answers will vary. Possible answers:
17. Las chicas
18. El banco/la tienda
19. don Carlos
20. La panadería
21. Benito
22. doña Anabel

Alternative Quiz 9-2A

A. (12 points: 1.5 points per item)
1. más largo que
2. tan bonita como
3. más estrecha que
4. más anchos que
5. tan caro como
6. menos cómodos que
7. más delgadas que
8. menos amables que

B. (7 points: 1 point per item)
9. C
10. D
11. D
12. D
13. C
14. D
15. C

C. (16 points: 2 points per item)
16. el par de botas
17. el dependiente
18. los probadores
19. la cajera
20. la caja
21. la cliente
22. el escaparate
23. la etiqueta

Alternative Quiz 9-3A

A. (18 points: 2 points per item)
1. i
2. c
3. a
4. g
5. e
6. h
7. f
8. b
9. d

B. (9 points: 1.5 points per item)
10. c
11. a
12. b
13. b
14. c
15. a

C. (8 points: 2 points per item)
16. Los compró para su tía Azucena.
17. La compró para su abuela.
18. Lo compró para su tío Eduardo.
19. Las compró para su mamá.

CAPÍTULO 9

Answers to Alternative Quizzes 10-1A, 10-2A, and 10-3A

Alternative Quiz 10-1A

A. (10 points: 1 point per item)
1. se casó
2. me perdí
3. se durmió
4. leyó
5. se enamoraron
6. se cayó
7. creyeron
8. se rompieron
9. se despidieron
10. se fueron

B. (12 points: 2 points per item)
11. Hacía; se perdió
12. Eran; llamó
13. desayunaba; recibió
14. vio; íbamos
15. dormían; oyeron
16. se sentía; llegaron

C. (8 points: 1 point per item)
Answers may vary. Possible answers:
17. c, d
18. a, c
19. a
20. c
21. c, d
22. a, c
23. d
24. b

Alternative Quiz 10-2A

A. (24 points: 2 points per item)
1. eran
2. decidió
3. se fue
4. dormían
5. se levantó
6. hizo
7. hacía
8. estaba
9. vio
10. llegó
11. llamó
12. se abrió

B. (6 points: 1 point per item)
13. la estrella
14. el príncipe
15. la princesa
16. el OVNI
17. el planeta
18. la galaxia

C. (5 points: 1 point per item)
19. C
20. E
21. C
22. C
23. E

Alternative Quiz 10-3A

A. (9 points: 1.5 points per item)
1. tuve
2. tuvieron
3. tuvo
4. tuvo
5. tuviste
6. tuvimos

B. (12 points: 1.5 points per item)
7. T
8. R
9. R
10. R
11. R
12. T
13. T
14. T

C. (14 points: 2 points per item)
15. chisme
16. rompieron
17. furioso
18. chismosos
19. noticias
20. metiche
21. hicieron las paces

Answers to Alternative Quizzes 11-1A, 11-2A, and 11-3A

Alternative Quiz 11-1A

A. (6 points: 1.5 points per item)
Answers will vary. Possible answers:
1. No, nadie está preocupado por la situación.
2. No, mis amigos nunca tratan de reciclar.
3. No, no hay ninguna solución al problema del smog.
4. No, no podemos hacer nada por la playas contaminadas.

B. (12 points: 1.5 points per item)
5. contaminación
6. tira
7. químicos
8. selvas
9. destrucción
10. capa
11. desperdicio
12. combustibles

C. (12 points: 2 points per item)
13. a
14. e
15. d
16. f
17. c
18. b

Alternative Quiz 11-2A

A. (14 points)
1. El águila calva
2. El oso pardo
3. El águila calva
4. El oso pardo
5. El delfín
6. La tortuga marina
7. El delfín

B. (9 points: 1.5 points)
Answers will vary. Any choice here is correct.

C. (12 points: 2 points per item)
14. a
15. b
16. a
17. a
18. b
19. b

Alternative Quiz 11-3A

A. (15 points: 1.5 points per item)
1. resolver
2. cambiar
3. mantener
4. tirar
5. reciclar
6. proteger
7. evitar
8. conservar
9. apagar
10. desesperarse

B. (10 points: 2 points per item)
11. Vamos
12. Desfilemos
13. Hagamos
14. Organicemos
15. Escribamos

C. (10 points: 2 points per item)
16. Si trabajamos juntos, vamos a resolver los problemas.
17. Si compramos menos productos empacados, vamos a tener menos basura.
18. Si no cuidamos las especies, van a desaparecer.
19. Si usamos menos los carros, vamos a tener menos smog.
20. Si no dejamos de contaminar los lagos y ríos, no vamos a tener agua limpia.

Answers to Alternative Quizzes 12-1A, 12-2A, and 12-3A

Alternative Quiz 12-1A

A. (9 points: 1 point per item)
1. Querido
2. gracias por
3. te echo
4. sabías que
5. siguen
6. dale un saludo
7. noticias
8. abrazo
9. cariño

B. (12 points: 2 points per item)
10. Deberían encontrar empleo.
11. Debería montar en tabla de vela.
12. Debería hacerse amigo de sus vecinos.
13. Debería quedarse con sus parientes en Santo Domingo.
14. Deberíamos quedarnos en un albergue juvenil.
15. Debería quedarse en casa.

C. (14 points: 1 point per item)
16. te quedaste; Encontraste
17. fue; asistió
18. hizo; compró
19. corrimos; pasamos
20. acamparon; se hicieron
21. viajaron; escalaron
22. fui; aprendí

Alternative Quiz 12-2A

A. (8 points: 1 point per item)
1. buena gente
2. nos llevamos
3. lindísimo
4. quedé impresionado
5. está rodeado
6. clima
7. seco
8. bastante

B. (10 points: 2 points each)
9. le cayó
10. te cayeron
11. me cayó
12. le caímos
13. les caí

C. (12 points: 1.5 points per item)
14. tenía
15. nos llevábamos
16. éramos
17. dormía
18. nos despertábamos
19. encantaba
20. decían
21. cuidaba

Alternative Quiz 12-3A

A. (14 points: 2 points per item)
1. cierto
2. falso
3. cierto
4. falso
5. cierto
6. falso
7. falso

B. (12 points: 2 points per item)
Answers will vary slightly. Possible answers:
8. Cuando terminen las clases, voy a descansar mucho.
9. Cuando ella tenga más dinero, mi hermana mayor me va a comprar un carro.
10. Cuando vuelva al colegio en septiembre, voy a tomar muchas clases difíciles.
11. Cuando mi amiga Verónica tenga tiempo, va a visitarme.
12. Cuando lleguen mis primos, nosotros vamos a divertirnos mucho.
13. Cuando encuentre un empleo, voy a comprar una computadora.

C. (9 points: 1.5 points per item)
14. vamos a ir
15. va a visitar
16. voy a tomar
17. vas a recibir
18. vas a hacer
19. van a quedarse